AF483258

A TRUE STORY OF THE PANDEMIC CHRONICLES

MY DAD'S DAUGHTER

A GIFT TO MY HERO IN HEAVEN

DIVYA GUPTA KOTAWALA

ISBN. 979-8-88555-477-0

In the memory of my beloved father

Shri Suresh Gupta

"Dad"

You are remembered every time I smile

Contents

Dad *7*

Remembering Suresh – A Friend, Philosopher and Guide *10*

Preface *13*

Acknowledgement *19*

1. Dealing with Death 23
2. My Dad's Daughter 31
3. My Dad, the Family Man 49
4. Dad, the Rock Star 64
5. Dad's Endless Love for His *Alma Mater* 81
6. And COVID Hits Us Bad 96

7. The Ordeal Began 113

8. Our Last Goodbye Was Never Said! 128

9. Farewell 139

10. Celebrating Dad 152

11. The New Me 185

12. The Show Must Go On… 200

Author Bio *217*

Epilogue *219*

Dad

(Protagonist)

My dad, Shri Suresh Gupta, the main protagonist of this book, is also the main character in my life.

My father was an extraordinary man in this ordinary world. He was a giver, and he believed in maintaining strong and lasting relationships with everyone around him, be it his family, extended family or an extremely vast network of friends. He was the best friend anyone could ever ask for, a true people's person, so warm and humble.

He had won several hearts with his warm smile and tight hugs of care and love. He was a very well-educated and well-aware person. He had studied on government scholarship at Modern School, Barakhamba Road, where he was an outstanding student all throughout and excelled in studies and extracurricular activities. Later, he joined the prestigious St. Stephen's College and completed his bachelor's with honours in Economics. Thereafter, he got his MBA degree from Delhi's Faculty of Management Studies (FMS).

In the 1970s, he became the first entrepreneur in his family of seven siblings. With his hard work and commitment, he was able to bring fumigation machines from Germany and the United States (US) to India for the first time. As long as he lived, he was always ready to try new things and take risks. For him what always mattered was experience and relationships; money always came second. No wonder he gave everything with a large heart and hands full whenever anyone approached him for help and guidance.

My dad was a true example of a family man, faithful husband, caring friend, loving father, perfect businessman and, most importantly, an exceptional human being who truly deserved to be celebrated. This precious life was lost to COVID in 2021, as it hit his family and he was left to deal with the most challenging circumstances alone. Even in that situation, his family's safety was his only priority.

His sudden demise left many shocked and shattered. Losing a loved one is difficult, but COVID made the pain and the ordeal even more unimaginable. Someone who always spread so much love, happiness and positivity all around with his generous gestures left in such silence that it was unbelievable for many.

A man like him can never be forgotten. It is from this thought this book, *My Dad's Daughter*, was born.

The book is for him, he is the hero and every page of this book will talk about his life, his journey and his values, and by doing so, it will always keep him alive, spreading the strong fragrance of his aura around and cherishing his memories for years to come!

Those who we love, don't go away; they walk beside us every day, unseen, unheard, but always near, still loved, still missed and very dear.

Dad

Dad and Me

Remembering Suresh - A Friend, Philosopher and Guide

My earliest memory of Suresh is of playing hockey on the fields of Modern School. He was several years senior to me. He remains etched in my mind as one of those who excelled in academics sports and extracurricular activities. Suresh was a Prefect in school and the care, affection and warmth he showed left a huge imprint on his juniors. In many ways, he was a quintessential Modernite, full of energy and dynamism and would fill anyone up with the same spirit who came in touch with him.

When I joined St. Stephen's College in 1973 to pursue economics honours, he was graduating out of the college that very year. He went that extra mile to ensure that we, the new kids from Modern School, were comfortably settled and not harshly ragged in the college. His spirit of camaraderie, his jovial nature, his love for bonding with school and college mates, and his tendency to always assist and support remained his hallmark throughout his life.

When I made it into the IAS, Suresh was one of those few who celebrated it by inviting a few close friends. This was his way of saying that he was always there for me. He was a very generous host. This practice of regular bonding eventually became a way of life for him. When I got posted at Delhi and during my subsequent tenures, the only way and the fastest route to catch up on what was happening across India was to meet Suresh and join him in his monthly lunch, which was very special and restricted to only a few selected Modernites and Stephanians. He was always full of warmth and generosity. He never allowed anyone else around him to foot the bill.

He and Anju always remain an integral part of our lives. They were like family, the only few people you could fall back on for assistance and support in moments of need, no matter how big or small they were. Suresh was always there with his smile, his large heart and his desire to find a solution for all the problems that anyone close to him ever faced.

He was an extremely successful entrepreneur, and he always believed in creating wealth. He was always ready to help the poor, the downtrodden and those going through a tough time in life. He looked at life as an opportunity presented to him by God to help and assist others. In the same spirit, he continued to support every single good cause that ever came his way, especially those related to his school and college friends. The institutions he had studied in gave him a lot of pride and happiness, and he always had a burning desire to give back to these institutions in whatever possible way he could. He did all of this and so much more with his large and loveable heart than what many people with more wealth and resources could ever think of doing.

I still recall that time in my career when I was in Kerala I had found myself in a major problem with the communist government. It was one of the toughest periods of my official career. The comfort that came from Suresh calling me every single day, inspiring and motivating me was one of the rarest qualities of his personality that I admired. You could always count on him and always fall back on him as he was the perfect friend, philosopher and guide in any moment of crisis.

Suresh Gupta is no more with us today. Tragically, he became a victim to the pandemic. Despite our best effort, we could not save him. His memories will continue to spread fragrance in our lives for many years to come. His positivity, enthusiasm and commitment towards any relationship that he ever formed will continue to inspire and motivate us. He shall always be deeply missed by all those whose lives he had touched and became a part of till the very end. His going away left a huge void in our lives.

– Amitabh Kant

CEO, Niti Aayog

(Dad's close friend from Modern School and St. Stephen's College)

Preface

"*Yaaron ka Yaar*, Suresh, our dear friend was a live wire. He can never rest in peace, for wherever he is today, he will be rocking and kicking, as always!"

In the eyes of most of his friends, that is the image of my father, whom I suddenly lost one day to COVID during the second wave in Delhi in 2021. He was neither a superstar nor a celebrity, but he ruled over so many hearts and touched so many lives that it totally made him a rock star. His friends described him as a mover and shaker at every event as he would add so much life and energy wherever he would go!

All people go, but how they leave always stays with their loved ones. When such a loving person, so selfless, so pure, left so suddenly, it hit me hard. He had to go one day, but the way he left was unbearable and unacceptable.

"Don't send me to the hospital; I will never come back," dad had said to me when I was admitting him to the hospital after he had tested positive for COVID. Every time I close my eyes, even after months of losing dad, his words still haunt me.

Little did I know that five days later, those words would actually come true and we would lose him forever. How do I explain the feeling of losing a parent? It was the first time I was going through that excruciating pain in my life, and I didn't really know how to handle it or the feeling of extreme guilt of being unable to save a very precious, cheerful life that surely would have lived longer had the pandemic not hit us.

I share the sentiments of so many like us who went through the same fear and anxiety, and in fact, lost the battle even before they were ready to fight. More than the pandemic itself, the panic that took over with the never-ending media coverage, TV channels and "WhatsApp university" fast-track courses on COVID made life miserable for many like us.

My dad was no different; he was constantly surrounded by fear, panic and unwanted suggestions, and all I could see him manifest was terror. Once an outgoing person, highly social and fun-loving networker, he was now reduced to being a slave shackled to the confines of his so-called safe environment — his house — which eventually failed to protect him.

But again, we were not the only ones to go through this tragedy. He was not the only life lost to COVID, and I was not the first daughter in the world to have lost her dear dad in the most challenging circumstances. I was not the only one to struggle to see their dad's smiling face for one last time, or cry incessantly for not being able to touch or hug him for the last time, or wait to console my mother for 15 days after losing dad as she was COVID-positive too. Yes, definitely not the only one, but unfortunately, one of the miserable ones!

And then, some may ask why a book to share my grief?

My dad was not known to all; he wasn't a celebrity. Then why does his story deserve to be told, or how can it help or heal another person? Why would anyone feel my pain or relate to it?

I say, why not? Life is the best teacher, and often an ordinary story can make you believe how extraordinary your life is. From struggle comes strength, even pain can be a wonderful teacher. When a daughter reflects on her otherwise routine life, ordinary experiences look extraordinary in retrospect. It is never too late to be grateful for something as ordinary as receiving a text message from your parents that says good morning.

When you actually face the brutal reality of death in the family, something in you breaks deep inside, and you can never ever be prepared to deal with it. I may not be capable enough yet to build a hospital in his memory, name a road after him or do something grand to keep his memories alive, but I can definitely do something special as my final send-off for someone who was truly a gift in my life; writing this book was my way to show my love for him. I believe every human being is unique and their journey can teach us a lot. In telling my dad's story, even if I can touch one life, help anyone heal or grow with my dad's experiences or shortcomings, I would feel my purpose is achieved.

A father's love often goes unacknowledged, and his efforts are taken for granted. However, their importance in a child's life is immeasurable. It is a relationship that can never be replaced. Parents are our first family; we always look to them for help, love, guidance and support. Losing dad felt as if the umbilical cord connecting my heart to dad's was snapped away with brute force. We may choose to form any relationship again, be it of a soul sister or a *rakhi* brother, we may adopt kids or remarry, but there can be no other biological mother and father ever again.

Having said that, one cannot deny the fact that death changes everything and time changes nothing. With every passing day, I miss dad more and more; I miss the sound of his voice, the wisdom in his advice, the stories of his life, and I just miss his presence in every moment. Just as much today as on the day I heard the news of his passing away. So, time changes nothing! What it does change though is the way you process your grief. Your grief finds an expression over time.

This book is about every father like my dad; it is about the life he lived, memories he made, lives he touched. Even when he was being taken to the hospital, he was still so concerned about his friends and was thinking about their safety, and when I told him to think about himself, not others, he said, "every blessing counts, so keep collecting, keep helping." This book is about every daughter like me who may be extremely emotional, but that definitely doesn't make her weak. We, as daughters who are married, are affected the most by the anguish of losing our parents as we don't get to live with them always and the distance hits us the most at the time of such a separation. It is about our father–daughter bond that today gives me the biggest strength to survive against all odds. It's about the love we humans look for in a relationships and yet, at times, take them for granted. It's about the endless and the most painful ordeal that all the COVID-hit families like ours went through and, most importantly, it's about how one deals with death and yet moves on without a choice. It's a question that maybe by now has been asked several times by so many like me — WHY US?

It is a tribute to my dad, who had the most charming smile, infectious energy, warmest hugs and a large heart; a true friend and a complete family man, and his journey through his daughter's eyes. It's about celebrating his legacy. The farewell he never got but truly deserved.

This book is a reminder that grief has two parts. The first is the loss and the second is the rebuilding of life all over again. It's about sharing that dark part of one's grief that brings a constant ache and reminds us that nothing can ever be the way it was before. We all have a different purpose, and it's all about finding it the right way and at the right time. It is about showing love before it's too late. It's about an incomplete goodbye of an extraordinary soul in this ordinary world. As it has been said, "sometimes you will never know the value of a moment until it becomes a memory," this book is about those endless memories that dad gave to his friends and family and to me. As his daughter, I want to hold on to all his memories and not let them fade away ever! We may lose a parent at any age, but their love remains unchanged and so does the throbbing pain of not having them around and dealing with a constant fear of not letting your parents eventually move to a different world distant from you. With the passage of years, his memories will begin to diminish; the book is an effort to always keep him around and alive in our hearts through the pages of this book for years to come, celebrating dad and the beautiful life he had lived.

And if with my *Guruji's* blessings I am able to touch a few lives with my book, help a daughter share her inner feelings with her dad before it's too late or motivate a father to live his life to the fullest without any regrets, even if I am able to make a difference in one precious life and help anyone realise the beauty of some special relationships that are irreplaceable, I'll feel my efforts were truly worth it and all my prayers that I want to send to my dad in heaven are answered.

To all the fortunate people, I have only this to say, "hold dear to your parents, for it's a confusing and scary world without them."

Acknowledgement

This journey began to give a befitting farewell and tribute to my father, whom I love and respect the most. My heart feels the same pain today as the book reaches fruition, as I felt on the day when I began writing. How I wish I had written a fairy tale or a love story with a happy ending rather than a tribute, but then, perhaps I would not have written at all.

"My Father didn't tell me how to live; he lived, and let me watch him do it."

– Clarence Budington Kelland

When I began writing, I was lost. As I coddiwompled, I found my father to be my guiding light. Every time I got stuck, I asked myself how my father would have dealt with it. I had the answer. Thank you dad, for leaving with me the most enriching guidebook – your life!

I feel grateful that you found me my partner – Manish – with whom I have a beautiful daughter – Manya – both of whom have been my pillars of strength and my biggest support systems during this emotional journey. They stood by me during what I would call the most devastating experiences of my life and they never gave up on me. They lived with me through this pain every day, week and months, quietly and strongly. For most, death in the family leads to a mourning period of few days or weeks, eventually life does get back to normal. For us a family of three, we lived it every day in this past 11 months with this book in making, a thank you feels just so small for what you both did for me and because of me. I must also acknowledge that in the process, Manya also became my guide, helping a technically challenge, emotionally distraught mother, with typing, formatting and cleaning the manuscript over and over again.

This book would have never been possible without the silent support and encouragement of my dearest mom Anju Gupta. I had never imagined that not only she would understand my deep unconditional love for my dad, but even help me in this journey whenever I needed her help and suggestions. I also thank her for letting me write this for the person, who belonged to her, more than anyone else.

There came a time when I was lost, had no direction and didn't know how to structure my book, being a first time author this whole process was not just too overwhelming, but also seemed adrift. Then entered my most special North Star, someone who not only guided me but also gave me so much strength and right direction, something needed that time. Someone I had never met, spoken to or even knew and then entered my new found friend Tanu Goyal whom I accidentally met at the MSOSA reunion in December 2021. My heartfelt gratitude to my now lifelong friend, Tanu, who'll always have a special place in my life.

Thank you to my friends and Dad's friends who actually knew about this book all this while. Not only did they tried helping me in their full capacity, but their kind words of encouragement gave me so much hope and helped me believe that I could actually reach the finishing line soon.

Last but not the least, I would like to acknowledge the efforts of the entire team of Notion Press who very patiently gave me the strongest hand to hold when I needed it the most. I would specifically like to thank Vishal, Yeshwini and Kush for bearing with my crazy queries, timeline, confused mind and emotional outbursts during the whole publishing process.

At times our own light goes out and is rekindled by a spark from another person. I thank each and every person that I mentioned for being that spark in my life and to even those whom I may have missed, this book will always remain my most valuable possession for life as it is about my Dad, his life, teachings and beliefs. Every time I will flip through the pages of this book a part of me shall always think of you all and will always keep you close in my prayers and my heart.

Acknowledging the good that you already have in your life is the foundation of all abundance. Moving forward in life with what I have and learning to live with what I lost, forever in gratitude.

1

Dealing with Death

"jātasya hi dhruvo mṛityur dhruvaṁ janma mṛitasya cha
tasmād aparihārye 'rthe na tvaṁ śhochitum arhasi"

Bhagavad Gita: Chapter 2, Verse 27

"Death is certain for one who has been born, and rebirth is inevitable for one who has died. Therefore, you should not lament over the inevitable," the Bhagavad Gita says.

Death is the biggest, yet the hardest truth to accept.

It is 26 September 2021, and it has been exactly four months and 14 days since I lost the most precious part of my life — my father. What can be a more cruel irony than the fact that I finally gathered the courage to sit and write down about dad, about myself on my first Daughters' Day today without him. As I get more and more overwhelmed with emotions and surrounded by my memories, I can't help, but accept the fact that this hasn't been easy, this has been the most painful time of my life. It doesn't get better or the pain lesser with time. One definitely doesn't just learn to live with pain each day; the healing might take days, weeks, months, perhaps years,

I don't know. It's a struggle each day, and I miss dad every time I breathe; I miss him every time I close my eyes. Every day when I sleep, I wake up thinking of that unfortunate day when I got that call from the hospital telling me that I had lost him. Every time I eat his favourite food, I miss him; every day when I take a shower, I cannot figure out what washes my face more, the water or my flowing tears. Everyday something reminds me of him that's related to his presence and makes me miss his absence even more in my life now onwards.

There are days when I stop to ask myself what's really wrong with me. Is it all okay? Is it all normal? Is this the way every daughter reacts upon losing her father? Am I taking it too badly? I ask myself a 100 questions with no answer in return. Yes, I loved my dad too much, but did I love him so much that today I can't love myself? I can't come to terms with his death, which I always knew would happen someday, and I will have to eventually deal with it, but I cannot take the way it happened. Even to begin to imagine life without him right now seems so impossible; every festival, every milestone will be so incomplete. As the head of the family, he always celebrated all of us and stood by us, tough as a big rock of support. He always encouraged us to the best of his capacity so that we become what we are today.

Death is inevitable, I agree, but losing dad to COVID brought an unimaginable pain. Dad was my biggest pride, and I always looked up to him, but today I'm lost. My heart misses the warmth of his love; there is a vacuum now that cannot be filled. So much was left unsaid, unheard and undone, and all because we were up against a seemingly invincible pandemic. For the rest of my life, I will miss his love and concern. What once felt like lectures and scolding, today my ears long to hear in his voice. There are losses that rearrange your world, death that changes everything and grief that tears you down, pain that transports you to a very different universe, even when everyone else around you thinks nothing much has changed.

I often wonder if one could ever be ready to face death. The universal truth remains unchanged: whoever has taken birth will one day die. So, why is it so tough to deal with it for some people? I guess it is the level of attachment and the degree of pain, which differ for all. Why do we celebrate and rejoice a birth so happily and turn to a long, dark period of mourning when there is a death? Grief turns out to be a place none of us know till we reach there. We all experience grief at some point or the other, even if the magnitude varies. We could always anticipate that someone close to us might die one day, but we never look beyond the immediate few days and weeks that follow after the loss. We even misconstrue the nature of those few days. We expect that if the death is sudden, what might follow is a sudden shock or disbelief, but what we never expect is a shock so obliterative and dislocating for both body and mind. We might get inconsolable and a bit crazy with the loss. We imagine that the moment that would most severely test us would be the funeral, after which this hypothetical healing might take place. But what actually happens is way beyond what anyone of us can ever imagine or be prepared for.

I often wonder what could be the right response to a loss. When we actually fail to get through this pain and rise to an occasion that might look to the outer world as a projection of strength, we try and behave in a manner that might make others feel we are doing okay and some around us might consider this as the correct way to deal with death of a loved one.

In simple words, what I felt upon losing dad was an inexplicable pain. A throbbing one that I felt in my stomach, in my heart and every inch of my body every night as I lay down lifeless, crying and thinking about what had actually happened, how it happened and, most importantly, WHY it happened.

We asked a lot of questions.

Where did we go wrong? Why couldn't we control it? How we could have dealt with it better? Did we take any wrong decisions?

All this and many more questions haunt me day and night. I miss him, I miss 'Us'. How could he leave like this? Perhaps he himself didn't know it was time to go. I did lose him, but he lost so much more in one moment! He lost all the relationships and left all alone. We stayed back, but he began a new journey, of which nothing is known. So many of his wishes remained unfulfilled, so many important works left pending and so much love remained unshared. It makes me so sad to think that my dad would never have wanted to leave like this; this was not the way he would have wanted to say the last goodbye. Dad would have wanted to leave in style, surrounded by people and their warmth and love. He would have wanted his absence to be felt, works to be remembered and to be celebrated every day.

No wonder his departure hit me so hard. This is not what he deserved being the wonderful man he was. As a daughter,

I failed to do anything for him for the last time. As I thought more and more about it for days, dealing with grief became tougher and, surprisingly, the strange idea of writing a note in the diary to him every day to ease my pain resulted in the idea of a book that I actually wanted to share with the world. Initially, it looked impossible as while writing, you tend to revisit the same experiences over and over again, and it surely does get painful to handle the emotions at times. Yet, the idea did not leave my mind. For the longest time, writing was easy as pen was always my friend. Ever since I was a child, I had found it easier to put down my emotions on paper. I have always loved writing down everything I observe or anything that I want to hold on to and remember later; making notes has always been a hobby, something that I can still do non-stop. That's surprisingly a lot of writing for someone who just can't sit to read books. Yes, as astonishing as it may sound, till now I have never ever read a single book, except academic books. Somehow, I have never had the patience to sit and actually read a book from start to finish. No matter how hard I tried, for me to get into someone else's space of thought was never easy.

So, how could someone like me think of writing a book? I guess emotions find their own way, and eventually, find a means of expression and communicate too. It's a constant struggle to hold on to each and every memory of dad and deal with the insecurity of losing his messages, chats, pictures and videos as now those are all I have of him. It is a painful realisation that now I will not have any new pictures or memories with him. I will grow old, but he will look the same. With every passing year, I will change, but we won't have new memories with him. I wanted to remember him in good and bad times and to simply keep him alive in my heart and memory for as long as I live, and writing a book was the best possible way for me. I remember the pain of always trying to zoom in on his last pictures that came from the hospital for days after I lost him and praying for him to wake up one last time so that this nightmare could end. It was tough as I wanted to share my pain, anger, grief, love and many more emotions that were associated with dad as well as attempt to give him the fitting farewell he truly deserved. I wanted to connect with him for one last time and say my final goodbye in my way, or maybe make him live forever among us through this book, like he never left. I needed to talk about what made him so special, not only in my life but in others' too. People do move on in life, what stays back are moments and how one made you feel during your highs and lows. Those people are truly special who are remembered even after they are gone as they continue to stay in everyone's heart and memories forever.

The idea to write not only gave me a window to vent out my emotions, but it also gave me a new purpose. Suddenly, this was my new way of connecting with dad every day. His unique way to communicate with me. As slowly life started going back to routine, this was my special time with dad, something that I would look forward to. It offered me time to chat with dad and about dad, to remember little things about his life, finding out details from everyone around and constantly making notes. This was my most-awaited time of the day when it would be just me, dad and our memories. I have lost count of how many times I had shed tears while writing, and as it happened on so many instances, I even got a big smile on my face remembering our beautiful times together. It made me realise how lucky I was to have him in my life and how unfortunate we were to lose him so soon.

And why not? After all, dad was super special, someone who I always thought was so perfect. He was famous and loved by so many, forever spreading his warmth and helping those in need and touching lives of anyone he met. As I sat down to think about him, it was time to walk down the memory lane, to live with him one last time. When I started writing, initially, I found it heavy and painful, and so much anger and resentment welled inside me. However, as I kept writing for days, I realised that there was so much more I could write. It's my way of telling people what he truly meant to me and sharing what so many people thought of him. How often do we tell people how much we love them? We always wait for the right moment, but it never comes. We take people for granted, until we realise they're gone; we lose the opportunity to show our love and tell them how special they were. This is my way of telling dad how proud I have always been of him. Perhaps, I never told him that. I forgot to tell him that this was the most giving relationship of my life where I always received so much love, guidance, blessings, gifts and values, and in return, nothing was ever expected. Losing him felt like losing the cosiest blanket of love and protection. Life will eventually go back to routine, but it will never be the same as I won't have him back ever again.

The pandemic has given us lessons of a lifetime. It touched almost everyone in this world and affected almost every family in some way or the other. The most unfortunate ones like us lost a loved one and many lost their jobs and means of livelihood, businesses were badly affected, companies and factories were shut down, relationships succumbed to the intense pressure of time and many failed after years of existence. Many realised that money cannot buy everything and all we wanted was food and basic amenities for a happy life, whereas some continued running the blind race amassing power and assets with no signs of ever stopping. On the whole, the pandemic brought extreme imbalance in the lives of people. Even today, as I watch the news, I sit and think of all the unfortunate events. When I see life slowly getting back on track for many after a long period of chaos and discomfort, it fills me with so much remorse that some losses, like ours, won't be recovered ever. It is like any war that happens and takes away so many precious lives. Eventually, all wars end and so will the pandemic as we all know nothing lasts forever, except the loss of a precious life. As the surviving soldiers return back home with the pride of victory over the enemy in the war, the families of the soldiers who lost their lives in the bargain would never ever be able to celebrate this triumph as the void created in their lives would never be filled, just like the COVID-hit families like us.

There are people who cannot hear about grief due to obvious reasons. It is unpleasant. Imagine the plight of those who are living with grief everyday. It demolishes you.

2

My Dad's Daughter

Dear dad, you held my hand for a little while but you will hold my heart forever!

The attachment of the first-born child in the family is always special and stronger and even more so when it's a girl.

I used to be always happy, forever smiling and cheerful and this trait of mine was often what people identified me with, but I never knew it was all because of you, dad. As long as I had you, nothing at all ever mattered, no problem ever seemed big enough to make me sad, no day was ever dull as I had your love and warmth with me. You are, you were and you will always be a part of my soul and my existence as long as I live. You were the greatest giver I knew, and all I ever wanted to give you was pride and happiness. But today, there is a gnawing hollowness in my chest. The worst of it all is the fact that I'll have to learn to live with it forever and deal with the emptiness that you left behind.

We shared a very beautiful bond — you forever being a sweet, concerned and super protective dad and me being the obedient, respectful daughter. There was nothing you ever said that I didn't obey and there was nothing I ever asked that you didn't give. But I wish you had fulfilled my last wish of not leaving me like this. You gave me my name, you gave me my existence, helped me complete every milestone of life. You were always a part of my conversation, the centre of my existence. You made me believe that simplicity wins over everything else and how a perfect life was to be lead. You gave me values that I shall always keep as my biggest treasure! People inherit property, jewellery, gifts and assets from their loved once after their demise. I feel proud to have inherited your teachings, principles and beliefs that shall live with me till my last breath.

Be the things you loved most about people who are now gone.

It's often said that daughters are special, but what truly makes them special is the love and protection they receive from their parents, even when they have grown up and married and have their own kids. As a human being, I might have several emotions and different reactions to different situations, but as a daughter, all I ever had was a lot of love and gratitude towards my parents. As a father, my dad fulfilled all his duties sincerely. As I walked down the memory lane, I could not help but think how many beautiful and memorable moments dad, whom I addressed as dad, papa or poppsy, had given us as a family. Nobody knows it better than my husband, to whom I have mentioned my father's perfections and valuable lessons so many times that by now he must be irritated listening to it. I have memories of seeing him at all my school parent–teacher meetings, sports days, family Sunday shopping trips and much more. He was always there when we needed him to guide us, to scold us and to protect us. As a daughter, I always respected this fact and appreciated this commitment that my dad showed towards us. I often tried my best to repay this love and affection by being respectful and obedient towards him. I might have got into many quarrels and arguments with my mother, but when it came to dad, there were just no questions ever asked. Dad was my hero, and I always looked up to him. So, I never gave him any opportunity to question me and tried my best not to ever upset him. Those who knew me knew it well that dad was the only person who could get anything done from me, the only one who could change my views and opinions when the rest would fail, that his words were my command. But that never meant I was scared of him. I did it because his opinion and suggestions were always special and important in my life. I was always so emotionally attached to him that I often used to cry at the drop of a hat, even if he would ever call my name loudly. As I grew up, this led to the foundation of a beautiful relationship between us that was based on love, trust and affection.

I always took a lot of pride whenever I was compared to my dad. We shared a lot of common views, interests and emotions; one such emotion was the love for our school and college. It was just so special to attend school and college events and reunions with him and share the same pride as he had for the institutions he had been to. He was so happy when my daughter joined the same school and carried forward his legacy of being a blue-blooded Modernite. Another common personality trait that we shared was the love of being with and being surrounded by friends. We both loved networking and maintaining beautiful bonds of friendships with anyone we came across on the path of life. Dad was always very happy and proud of me that I had followed in his footsteps in this regard.

Dad was special, someone who even back in the 80s had the vision to break the glass ceiling and have such a liberal and modern mindset that never supported any gender bias. From the very beginning, he never discriminated between me and my brother and offered equal opportunities to grow and get good education, which totally became the base of my upbringing and shaped up my present. He was modern, he was well-educated, he had seen the world and interacted with so many, when I was young I fell ill and was recommended a very high intake of protein in my daily diet. Being allergic to eggs since childhood, my dad made sure I was introduced to non-vegetarian food regardless of the fact that we belonged to a Hindu community where most didn't even eat onion and garlic. For him my health was the prime concern and nothing else mattered. He was always a typical dad (a super cute, possessive dad). Nothing could ever change him. I believe he must have started planning my wedding since the day I was born. Dad named me 'Divya', a name he loved. He would often call me Cheenu, my nickname, which always reminded me of the love of my parents. He was most instrumental in laying the foundation of the initial years of my growing up and deciding my educational qualifications. It was only because of his vision that I took my first baby steps inside my school, Modern School, and it was he who made sure that I joined his college, St. Stephen's College and carry forward his legacy. If I had gone by my mom's wish, I would have surely landed in an all-girls college for sure. Dad definitely gave me wings to fly, but he made sure that the strings attached to my wings were always in his control. Surprisingly, it never affected me for I never had to complain as I completely trusted his decisions. I grew up with deadlines and restrictions but still with a lot of love. In those days there were no mobile phones, so dad would park the car right outside the party venue sharp at 10 pm as he would not allow me to come back on my own, ever. And I was instructed to come out on time or else he would leave the venue and go back home. I remember I used to start looking at my watch 30 minutes prior to his arrival as I could never give him a chance to get angry. I remember the protective dad in him would not let me wear short dresses, never let me go for a school trip. On one such occasion, to make me miss my school trip, he actually took me for a shopping trip to Bangkok to make me happy. I was so upset at that time that I didn't even realise how much he loved me and was just being protective of me to not let me go alone as a young girl. As his only daughter, I was never given permission for sleep overs, late-night parties or such things. Even when my friends would tease me for it, I, as his obedient daughter, never complained or compared my situation with my friends'. Dad taught me to always be content and happy with what I had. His teachings has helped me stay grounded. He taught me to win things in life or simply wait for them if it wasn't the right time, and most importantly never to compare oneself with others or judge others as everyone has their own journey of life.

I often see a reflection of dad in me and my habits. Dad and I shared a love for food. In fact, we had very similar tastes. We both had a major sweet tooth, with our favourite being *moong dal* and *badam halwa*. Often during winter, he would ritually go all the way to our favourite food joint Kaleva at Connaught Place and get *badam halwa* packed for me and drop it with my guard and then call me up to eat and enjoy it. Even in fruits, we had such similar choices. We would both wait for the seasonal fruits such as mango and custard apple and would relish them so much together. Dad had this very peculiar habit: if he ever ate food very quickly, he would have non-stop hiccups, and we all used to make so much fun of him only to realise a few years later that I had developed the habit too! Today, every time my hiccups start, I get another reason to think of dad. We both loved butter chicken. Once, when mom was not around, dad told me to order butter chicken and *naan* and not tell mom as she would get angry due to dad's health concerns. We had the most amazing time together hogging some delectable butter chicken, *naan* and *gulab jamun*. I felt so scared and guilty for hiding it from mom as she was strict about dad's food habits, but today that one meal is one of the most beautiful memories I have with him. The taste of that food will always be in my mind and the happiness of spending that precious time together shall always be a cherished memory.

From selecting clothes to deciding my education, he helped me with every small and big decision of my life, even in choosing my life partner Manish. Dad took almost every major decision of my life. He was always very excited about my marriage. In fact, thanks to him, for the longest period of time the profession I wanted to take up when I was in school was to get married and become a housewife. I do at times regret not being a working woman or financially independent when I got married, but I guess that's what was planned for me. I trusted dad completely. Dad was both fun and strict when needed. He was the perfect combination of a modern, yet traditional father. He never encouraged me to drink, and I'm sure would not have liked it if I did, but he was the first person who made me taste alcohol when I started attending parties alone to ensure I was intelligent enough to choose my drinks. In fact, dad himself would host numerous parties for our friends in school and college and made sure that everyone had a good time. I still clearly remember one occasion when we decided to cancel the party as we knew that my friends would want alcohol to be served, but dad very coolly gave us the permission to set the bar on the condition that he would serve the drinks himself to all our friends. That was such a clever move from my dad; even though the party had a perfectly loaded bar with the best alcohol, none of my friends had the courage to ask dad for a glass of drink. That day I realised how smart my dad was.

We used to love Sunday shopping days with dad. For a long time, all my clothes were always selected by him. In fact, if he liked a design or a pattern on me, he would make sure I picked up all the colours of the same design available on the shelf. On one of my trips to Bangkok, he actually made me pick up every pair of footwear and bag in every possible colour I could think of. However, the best memory of his shopaholic nature remains the one time when I had demanded my first branded bag from him on my eighteenth birthday. As dad always felt I was the less demanding child of the two, he made sure to fulfil my every wish. So, on my eighteenth birthday, dad happily took me to the Louis Vuitton showroom at the Oberoi Hotel where I selected my bag and he happily bought it for me. At that moment, the shopaholic dad in him woke up, and he told me to pick the other colour of the same bag and finish it in one go for the next two years! The sales person at the showroom had the most amazing reaction when it seemed to him like that dad wasn't buying a branded bag, but was out for grocery shopping.

I am a big Shah Rukh Khan (SRK) fan, so all of us had gone to watch his latest movie at Chanakya. In those days, it was a trend to buy tickets in black. Without checking, my dad had paid a big amount for the movie tickets, and upon getting the money, the seller simply ran away. On hearing this, I got very upset and started crying. However, almost immediately, my dad found another man and bought new tickets in black and handed them over to me, saying that I didn't need to worry and just enjoy the movie. It brought a huge smile on my face and we enjoyed the rest of our evening with our popcorn and coke and SRK ofcourse.

Dad was also very sensitive towards others' feelings and emotions. I remember when I was in school, I had lost my Prefect badge in class 12th. I called up home and began howling badly. My mom didn't understand my feelings and scolded me for being so childish, but dad drove all the way from Ashok Vihar where we stayed in those days to school to pick me up and consoled me. Later, he even fought with the school management as he knew it was an injustice, as he knew I truly deserved it for the amount of hard work I had put in as a dedicated and hardworking student to win it but lost it due to some category clash issue. However, when the school offered to give the badge to me later, he asked me to turn it down. He felt that my friends would never understand it and make fun of me assuming I used dad's connection to buy it and he would have never liked it that way. I remember him telling me that he had got my honour back, but now I should return the badge and learn a lesson for a lifetime. In fact, years later, I found out from his batchmates that dad had gone through the same experience of almost losing the same badge. And he had fought for it until it was returned to him as he and his friends truly believed that he deserved it.

He used to feel very happy that I had acquired his skills of networking and love for staying in touch with people for life; however, stories about the same experiences used to leave mom irritated and she would often invoke God's help to control this crazy father–daughter duo whenever we would sit and enjoy our chat sessions over the same topic. Dad taught me the value of being humble and generous. He believed that one warm smile could help you win a 100 battles. He made sure that we as kids learnt never to judge anyone by their social status and treat everyone equally and with respect. I would always try to be the little version of him and follow whatever he taught me in his lifetime.

I always received a lot of appreciation and encouragement from him; he was my biggest cheerleader. He always took so much pride in me for being a hard working student and would always scold me whenever he caught me studying late at night. When I was in standard 12, I had taken physical education as my sixth subject to improve my score for college; however, I somehow could not manage it among other kids, who were much better than me. Dad came to my rescue and helped me in all possible ways and because of that I passed that exam with flying colours. He was instrumental in helping me clear a very tough interview for my college admission, where eight students were competing for one seat. I got through only because of him as he had prepared me for it himself. I still remember my first day of college when I went back home with loads of books from the library, he laughed at me and told me I should rather enjoy the good food at the college *café* instead of studying so much.

After passing out from the National Institute of Fashion Technology (NIFT), I joined a famous designer duo for my internship. One day, dad came to pick me up and it turned out to be my last day at work because he found the surrounding area unhygienic and unsafe for his darling daughter to work. He was concerned that just like him I too had an extremely sensitive skin and would get reactions quickly if surrounded by dust or anything unhygienic. That was another similarity between us! Mom would always call the both of us delicate darlings, seeing us in trouble for the same reason so often.

I was my daddy's princess, and he gave me all the care and protection he could. No wonder I feel that vacuum so much that I believe that no other relationship can ever fill this void in my life. I had been so used to his handholding at every stage of my life that today it feels so empty and alone without his guidance and suggestions, even today when I get stuck in any decision making my heart looks for him everywhere.

Marrying me off to a good guy was one of his biggest dreams, and he definitely left no stone unturned to make the day larger than life in every possible way. He very clearly instructed mom during my pre-wedding shopping that anything I wanted be given to me. Everything was selected with so much love and care. He was involved in every little detail that concerned my wedding, from selecting the best Ravish Kapoor wedding card to my favourite red colour *lehnga* to his favourite venue at the Oberoi for the cocktail to the best food and floral arrangements. Everything we did had so much involvement from his side and that made the wedding all the more special. Being the protective dad that he was, he would get so upset every time I went out on a date with Manish that he would find excuses to not let me go. He would often say that eventually I would live with Manish so I should spend more time with him before I got married.

Dad got unwell a few days before my wedding, and as everyone in the family knew of dad's attachment with me and his excitement for the wedding, they all suggested I maintained a little distance from him so that his health didn't get further affected. However, on the final day, when I entered the main venue all dressed up as a bride, my dad became so emotional that he broke down the moment he saw me as he realised it was finally the time for me to leave. On my *bidaai* (Indian custom of saying goodbye to the daughter), he cried like a kid and was inconsolable. The warmth in that special hug that he gave me that day shall remain in my heart forever.

My wedding and the resulting physical distance changed so much between us that it became tough to make up for lost time, even in these past 15 years. What followed the wedding was limited interactions, fewer visits and occasional talks. Even though I always stayed close to him, this distance never ended. Even today, I fail to understand how and why despite the lack of discrimination and increasing stress on equal opportunity by today's parents, a girl's involvement, acceptance and importance drastically reduces in her maternal home post her marriage. Although this didn't come as a shock to me as I was always mentally prepared for the same, this distance always bothered me. It was definitely not one-sided; just as the maternal home prepared itself to see me less often, on occasions similarly, my new family and my daughter kept me busy enough. I believe that married daughters definitely have a tougher time as her grief of losing her parents is surely more painful and difficult to handle. After being already separated from my parents years back — I lost my family physically years ago on my wedding day — now I lost my dad emotionally too.

I remember how I used to wait to spend quality time with him post my wedding. Once on our family trip to Dharamshala, few years back, I woke up at 6 am on a holiday to go on a walk with dad so I could spend some time alone with him, catch up with him and just be with him. Throughout out trekking trip, dad scolded me for not being energetic and fit enough as I was all breathless while walking. He lectured me throughout the way, but later we had so much fun over a hot cup of tea and delicious *chola bhatura* together. The wait to be able to spend more time with my dad would now never end. I wish I could hug him one last time and tell him what he truly meant to me and how special he was and how much I used to look forward to always be with him.

Although there were many traits that made my dad unique and stand out from the rest, one very special trait of his was that his dictionary didn't have the word 'No'. He was always willing to help, give a suggestion or at least was ready to hear you out, and for every small or big demand that I ever made, the answer was always a YES. He was my forever Santa Claus, always showering me with love and affection. But this giving attitude was not just for me but for everyone who looked up to him with love and respect, there were many like me who often got showered with his generosity regardless of the fact whether they valued it or not, dad remained unchanged and unaffected.

His love and concern had no boundaries or limitations. Often, his love could not be seen but could only be felt in his words and his actions. I still remember, in the year 2009, when I went through a family split at my in-laws', dad was very concerned and tensed about me and my family's well-being. Although he stayed out of it that too only on my request, he was extremely miserable at home. Mom later told me how badly he sobbed the day I stepped out with my immediate family from the house on a path that was unsure and undecided, for that day he blamed himself for taking the biggest decision of my life without even asking me. Years later though I am very happy that he had no complaints seeing Manish as my life partner and felt proud every time he saw us together sharing our responsibilities together.

Dad was always very involved in our lives and it made our relationship so beautiful and special. I would often talk to him about matters that I thought would get me a scolding from mom. I remember an instance when I had to visit the Nizamuddin Dargah with a group of friends and I was very excited about it. Around the same time, there were certain terrorist attacks in Delhi and mostly around that area. I knew mom would have never given me permission even though my husband had no issues, but I wasn't able to go without informing her as my conscience didn't allow it. So, I told dad and asked for his permission. He understood my wish and gave me the permission on the condition that I stayed in touch with him until I got back home. The whole time I was out, he kept calling me and messaging me to keep a track of my whereabouts until I reached home safely. Later, he told me not to tell mom about it to avoid facing her anger. Once, I went to Chandni Chowk for some work-related shopping; for as long as I was out there, he made mom keep calling me to check on me out of concern for my safety and security. Just a few months ago my daughter had to go through some important medical tests. My dad could not even take one morsel of food till she was done with the tests and was safely out of it. Even when we travelled, his care travelled with us. On a trip to Paris once when Manish, Manya (our daughter) and I had gone to Disneyland, dad was overwhelmed with worry when we told him that we were doing the roller coaster ride. My super cute dad was so concerned about our safety he even joked that Manya and I had become daring and strong like the 'Kotawalas' and were not delicate like the 'Guptas' anymore. Wherever we went my dad's concern and love always followed us.

We always take our dear parents for granted when they are around. We never really feel the need to value their love and concern, but only when we lose them forever this realisation hits us and we learn how irreplaceable they were in our lives and that there won't be anyone ever like them who could love us so unconditionally and selflessly. So, tell them how much you love them before it is too late. Love your parents as much as you can, for one day they shall be in heaven and you won't be able to do the little things that you can today. Just like us, how we feel today for waiting for that right time that never eventually came for me or my dad, on his last birthday with us last year on 12th March 2021, as Delhi had started to open up and life was getting back to routine surprisingly on the 12th itself I had a few social commitments, but as dad's birthday was my priority I asked about his plans first. Dad had taken his first vaccination shot on 11th March and was a bit low. My brother was also buzy and a comfortable time wasn't being decided for all of us to meet and celebrate together. Due to this I got a little irritated as I had to plan my day accordingly. When I showed my resentment to dad he messaged me to go ahead with my plan and said he will enjoy the day his way, and why trouble anyone at all as his birthday comes every year! Even today my heart feels so sad that had I known it was dad's last birthday with us, I would not have troubled him at all and held him so tight to not let him go away. Even though we did eventually celebrate together and it was just so beautiful, this conversation on that day shall always leave me in a lot of pain every year when his birthday comes.

"A thousand moments I had just taken for granted, mostly because I assumed there would be a thousand more."

Dad and me in younger days

My Wedding

With Dad on his last birthday: 12th March 2021

Dad, Manya and Me

Mom, Dad, Manish and Me

3

My Dad, the Family Man

For every daughter, her father will always be her hero, and I was no exception to this rule. By nature this relationship is the most giving and loving of all, but there was so much more that made dad so unique. I want the world to know about him and remember him the same way I do in years to come and keep him alive in our thoughts. My dad was a simple man with big dreams, but he was always attached to his roots. For him, family was always the first and most important priority. Family was something which he could never ever compromise. Regardless of how social and outgoing he was, we never heard or saw him miss any of the family commitments. Not only did he love his family a lot, but he also touched the lives of each and every family member, who belonged to three different generations, and that is what made him so special and loved.

The youngest of seven siblings, born on 12 March 1953, in a simple and humble household in Jaipur, my dad was the most lovable and helpful of all, and I don't say this just because I was his daughter; I say this based on what I had seen and experienced during all these years I spent with him. The kind of commitment he showed and the involvement he had with each and every family member is something that is missed by each and every one of them. He always took part in their happiness and sorrow and was always ready to give whatever he could to make everyone's life happy and comfortable. In a family with so many members, I found it amazing how dad would never miss anyone's birthday or anniversary and always made it a point to wish them and send his love. He was their Google and the phone-a-friend pal; everyone would look up to him for suggestions. In his family, the one person that he was most attached to and loved the most as long as he lived was his father Shri Haripat Rai Guptaji, whom he fondly called *Bauji*! Dad lost him at a very early age and was deeply affected by this loss for a very long time. Mom used to often tell us that he used to miss his father a lot and took a very long time to recover from this loss. *Dadaji* was dad's biggest strength and backbone during his young age and gave dad the strongest values and upbringing that made him what he was for the world.

The bond between dad and *dadaji* was so strong that even in his last moments *dadaji* only waited to hug dad and shower him with his unconditional love and blessings. Losing *dadaji* was one of his biggest griefs as he always wanted and dreamt of giving his father a beautiful life full of all possible comforts and luxuries that a person like him truly deserved. Dad used to believe that he flourished only because of his father's blessings and support and that made him never look back or regret in life. In fact, even after almost 38 years of losing his father, dad had always kept *dadaji* alive in his heart, in his memories, his home and office with his beautiful pictures, which he would worship the first thing in the morning. It was a custom that he followed until his last breath. He initiated several awards in his school and college in his memory to keep him alive. He was equally concerned for and attached to his mother. He tried his best to give her all the comforts of life till she lived. Dad also shared a very beautiful bond with his father-in-law Shri Kuber Chandra Agarwal, a very respected and reputed businessman of Kanpur in those days. My *nana* (maternal grandfather) was one of dad's most favourite people ever. Dad had a lot of respect for him. He was the only person whom dad looked up to after losing his own father at a young age; he would often look up to him for advice and suggestions. *Nanaji* was not only a very humble and helpful person, but also an amazing human being. His death was also something that left a huge impact on dad as he always missed his guidance and warmth.

Apart from many others, one relationship that he held very close to his heart was the one he shared with my father-in-law Shri Ashok Kotawala. The bond they shared had nothing to do with me and my husband Manish at all. They had been friends for more than 30 years before we got married. Regardless of all the ups and downs in the relationship with the in-laws common in a marriage, they remained friends until my father-in-law's death six years ago. Dad was very fond of Ashok papa, and not even for a second in my married life of 10 years did he behave and treat Ashok papa as his *samdhi* (daughter's father-in-law). In fact, dad was always very straightforward and honest with him and always treated him as his dear friend. They would often meet for drinks at the NSCI club and talk their heart out; they always had a good time together. Although they had been introduced by common friends and relatives years ago, they remained good and loyal friends till the end. Dad did not even think for a second before promising his only daughter to Ashok papa's house when my marriage proposal came; he trusted him blindly. Not only were they business associates, but they also shared a bond that was beyond many people's understanding.

When Ashok papa tragically passed away in 2015, due to a sudden heart attack, dad was badly shaken. He had not only lost a dear friend but also a confidant whom he always trusted and valued. The people who saw dad at papa's prayer meeting saw the shocked friend and even suggested that he should be looked after well so he could cope up with the big loss. As long as dad lived, he cherished the beautiful times he had spent with Ashok papa and missed him on many occasions. He would often mention him, especially when there was any discussion about diamonds and good food like *dal batti churma*. Ashok papa would often get *dal batti churma* prepared for dad. He would often invite dad to his office for lunch as dad never bought jewellery from anyone else but papa because he trusted his knowledge and expertise in the field of jewellery blindly. These were among the few highly cherished relationships in dad's life that had earned a great amount of love and respect in his heart, even though he unfortunately lost them very soon and early in life, dad continued to treasure them in his life till his very end.

Dad was always everyone's most favourite uncle — *chachaji*, *mamaji*, *nanaji* and *dadaji*. The way he bonded with his nieces, nephews, brothers and sisters and with everyone in the family was truly commendable. After he left, they all had numerous stories and experiences to share about him that made him so special in their lives, to the extent of reaching out to him first for suggestions and guidance among all the seven siblings. One of his nieces once told me how loving dad was as a maternal uncle. Back in 1970s there were fewer resources and dad wasn't financially independent, yet he never missed an opportunity to spend time with the kids of the family and pamper them to the best of his capability.

When Pandit Jawahar Lal Nehru was visiting the Red Fort and the kids wanted to greet him, dad happily took two kids one on each of his shoulders all the way to Red Fort and fulfilled their wish. Once, he even took them all the way to the Taj Mahal in Agra and bought them pretty little trinkets as a token of his love, and they still remember it so fondly. It wasn't about the gifts, it was the love dad shared with each one of them that they miss so much. He connected with everyone with love, affection and a fun attitude, irrespective of their age groups, and it made him popular and loved among everyone.

He was always ready with a helping hand for anyone in need. Whether it was helping with school admissions, job transfers, clearing job interviews, passport or visa issues, any government-related works, promotions or organising family weddings and family reunions, dad took the first step and got everyone together. Even though he was the youngest of all, I saw him as the boss, a position that he had earned. He always made decisions keeping everyone in mind and held everyone in the family together. With him every occasion was full of life and memorable and all the arrangements would just be perfect because he used to execute most of them himself. Even today, his family misses his presence. Each one of them has stories to share about how dad influenced their lives, spent time with them and helped when they needed it. They remember him with so much fondness and they can't help mentioning how dad was one of the most sacrificing people ever. He always kept his family's and friends' interest before his own and often sacrificed a lot of his happiness and comfort for the same. There were many who even took advantage of his goodness and often took him for granted. However, these instances never made dad shy away from his responsibilities or loving them back in return. As long as he lived, he believed in the importance of family and did his best to uphold family values. That was my dad, a beautiful human being.

After marrying mom, Anju, a simple girl from a business family of Kanpur in 1979, dad began a new journey with her. The journey lasted for almost 41 years, leaving behind beautiful memories and experiences as well as learnings that they both shared as a couple and passed on to us to follow for the rest of our lives. Soon after, mom became the wind beneath his wings and his forever lucky charm. Together, they achieved many milestone in life and yet always kept themselves rooted to the ground and attached to family values. Mom and dad always complemented each other. As they continued the journey of life, I joined in as the first-born child on 13 January 1982, and then, my brother Dipesh on 23 December 1982. Yes, if you haven't noticed both the kids were born in 1982. It was something that God had planned for us as a family and got dad in so many confusions at various airports all over the world. The officers at the immigration would get confused as both kids were born in the same year in January and December, and dad would nicely explain them the joke that God had played with the Gupta family. His humorous take on this issue was bang on and remained intact!

One thing that never changed was Dad's giving nature, whether it was his family or his friends. Some people only come in your life to fulfil a purpose, some make your journey easy and some leave you, leaving behind lessons. Dad learnt and lived with so many experiences but the beauty of his life was that none of those experiences ever left him bitter or angry. He always moved ahead, learning his lessons or at times repeating the same mistakes again, yet never regretting. Not to mention the monetary help or emotional support he provided to so many without ever telling anyone else. The chilled-out trait of his would always help him deal with any situation or problem, no matter how big or small it was. He suffered every loss be it in business or relationships with grace and always moved ahead with the same energy and smile and never looked back with regret as he believed every experience left an important lesson, and if it didn't, then it was definitely not worth remembering.

He was a very loving grandfather to all the three grandkids of the family, Manya, Vedaanti and Veer. He showered the kids of the family with so much love and warmth and pampered them. I still remember the day my daughter Manya (the first grandchild of the family) was born, dad was so happy and excited. Being married in a conservative joint family, where the elders wanted a boy as the first child, I got so scared thinking about how they would react and started to cry upon hearing the news of my daughter's arrival. Dad got so upset with my reaction and scolded me. He asked me how I would have felt if he had given the same reaction the day I was born and that being so educated how could I even think like that. To cheer me up further, he even added that I should be happy that school admission for girl child would be easy as she would get a 5 percent weightage over the boys!

Over the years, he gave so much love to my daughter Manya and was proud of all of her little achievements. It gave him so much happiness the day she got through Modern School. He was literally on top of the world, seeing the third generation enter the school he had been to and shared this good news with many of his school friends. In fact, he played a vital role in laying the foundation of Manya's formative education, just like he had done for me. It was only because of him that my daughter got through Modern School that year, as she got extra points as her granddad was a Modernite too! And she got the benefit of generation points. A dream that my dad once saw for me, helped my daughter eventually, especially, in the years when school admission was getting so tough. Proud *nanu* would share his doll's (he often called her a doll with love) Kathak videos on his friends group and would later share all the responses with me with so much pride and happiness. He was the happiest when she cleared the exam and got through the famous Gandharva Mahavidyalay for Kathak dance.

The sweet bond that he developed with her is something that she would so badly miss for the rest of her life. He would get very angry with me every time I scolded her and would then pamper her in my absence. We had planned a family trip to Gulmarg, and unfortunately, at the airport due to some issue, the flight got cancelled. The kids were so upset that they all started crying and refused to go back home. Just at that moment, my dad surprised them by booking the flight to Goa instead and decided to go ahead with the trip as planned, the only change being that of the temperature, from minus 3 degrees to 35 degrees with the same luggage! It was definitely one of the most memorable and beautiful family trips for all of us thanks to our dear dad! This trip gave us memories for life that I shall cherish forever. Sometimes, we lose connect, move ahead in the race of life, fight or don't talk for long, but what always remain are memories that either bring a smile to our face or tears to our eyes. What eventually matter are the memories created, and dad surely left so many beautiful ones.

The kids in the family were always spoiled by him so much they would never ask anyone for anything when he was around, and all of their wishes, big or small, were easily granted. Every family trip as kids that we ever had left us with so many beautiful moments that can never be replaced. He took us to the US to show us Disneyland as kids. Even though he was terrified of roller coasters, that didn't stop him from making that first trip so memorable and super fun. He flew me to Paris just before my wedding as our last trip together. We were always his priority, to the extent that he and mom even dragged me along for their twenty-fifth anniversary trip to Malaysia as they refused to leave me back home alone! For a long time, I would not see my parents as a couple; they were always parents first. Our childhood on the one hand was filled with lots of comfort and warmth, yet on the other hand, nothing ever was given to us on a platter or was made easy until we had learnt our lessons right. Dad taught us to value money and never take it for granted; from earning our first pair of Reebok shoes to getting our first Swatch watch, not only did he make everything special, but also attached valuable lessons with it. On one of our very early trips abroad, we were with another family. As the funds for the trip could not reach dad in time, he told us not to shop much and keep a tab on our expenditure, to avoid any uncomfortable situation in front of his friend. But, as the immature kids that we were, we felt very bad as we were being teased by our family friend's kids for not being able to shop as much as them. Although dad felt bad, he maintained a calm self. In fact, he taught us the first and the most important lesson of our life — patience. As soon as we reached our next destination, the funds arrived and he gave us an open hand to do whatever we wanted and shop everything and even more from our list. He taught us to deal with every situation in life with lots of confidence, and if we ever lost it, we always had his support and suggestions by our side. The vast knowledge and experience that he had made it easy for us as kids and family to deal with any difficult situation at hand.

As a father-in-law to my husband Manish and Dipesh's wife Shagun, dad was equally loving and giving, for all one was ever expected to do was give respect to earn all his love and care. For years Manish and dad shared a very formal relationship, but after Manish lost his own father and did not receive much support from his own relatives, dad was forced to step into Manish's father's shoes to support and guide Manish whenever he needed it. Dad didn't even understand Manish's business nor did he ever get involved in it, but he was the only go-to person for Manish for mental and emotional support. In times of crises, dad became his backbone and gave him the courage to deal with the situation. Manish always felt that no matter how impossible the situation be, he would always have dad's blessings with him to deal with and win over the crisis. Dad was always proud of Manish for being a very hard working person, and he always appreciated his simplicity. Regardless of the fact that dad didn't agree with Manish on certain things and often got irritated, in the last few days Manish served him as his own son so selflessly when dad's own immediate family wasn't with him. I saw a lot of respect for him in dad's eyes and lots of gratitude. Today, Manish wishes that whatever little he could do for dad may always be with him as his blessings for the rest of his life.

Anyone who ever met dad or crossed path with him always remembered something good that dad had done for them. Although people have short memories and some even forget the good done to them or the help offered to them when it was most needed, one fact would never change and that is they would never find a replacement for a person like my dad in their lives ever. Because many things in life can be bought with money, but true bonds of human relationships, especially those of blood, are often irreplaceable. The giver that my dad was, he never turned back to see what he had lost or how he could have benefited himself. All he ever saw and believed was how he could help somebody in their hour of need. Even in his last few days before he left us, he stayed connected and attached to each and every family member he held close to his heart.

For dad, family was like music — some high notes, some low notes, but always a beautiful song!

Mom and dad's wedding picture with amma and bauji (dad's parents)

Mom, dad, Dipesh and me in younger days

Family of four

Dad with his full family

Dad with my nanu and nani (maternal grandparents)

Dad with shri Ashok Kotawala (my father in law)

Dad and his family

4

Dad, the Rock Star

Sometimes, we get so used to someone's smile that we fear seeing the tears!

Dad was full of life, happy-go-lucky and nothing less than a rock star. He made everything around him look so extraordinary and special. His personality and aura made him so attractive. And when I say this, don't think that it's the daughter's love speaking, for he really was special. No wonder so many people talk about his personality, even after he is gone. Some have even described him as the life of all events, parties and reunions. He was everyone's favourite. People would lovingly call him Suresh bhai. He had the warmest smile of all, a killer smile, if I may say so. It could literally win over anyone, from any age group. Even today when I meet anyone, the first thing they remember about dad is his smiling face and the tight affectionate hug he would give to most. Dad was a charmer; he added a unique spark to every get-together he was a part of and lighted up everything around him. He was gifted with a unique persona that left a lasting impression on anyone who met him. Those sparkling eyes and infectious energy added so much cheer and happiness to every occasion he was a part of. I can't help but admit that dad always enjoyed the limelight; he liked being famous, recognised and talked about. However, I must also admit that unlike many of us who like fame and enjoy it, dad was different as not only did he work hard to earn the fame that he truly deserved, but he also remained humble, helpful and attached to his roots. Speaking of dad, one of his friends had said, "Suresh didn't run after limelight, he remained humble enough to attract it with his deeds."

His fame and popularity among his friends and family definitely brought him a lot of happiness. His popularity ran across the globe amongst his school and college friends and many more, but it never resulted in arrogance. Dad was a multitasker; to him helping people didn't mean only charity, which he did very willingly and quietly, but meant much more in his book. He was always willing to extend a hand and get involved in organising things and events when needed. No reunion was possible without his involvement. Taking charge of things from selecting venues to menus, arranging the best alcohol for his friends in town or sponsoring passes and tickets, he loved doing everything on his own. To just dress up and attend a get-together is easy, but not everyone comes forward to volunteer to help in every possible way needed. But my dad was one of those who would never shy away from work, who would never run away from responsibilities, who would always come forward with suggestions whether they were welcomed or not.

He was resourceful; he could do anything from arranging chief guests at big events for his friends to suggesting event planners, caterers, venues for weddings or arranging singers for prayer meetings. I'm sure those of his friends and family who might be reading this would definitely resonate with my words and have a smile on their face remembering how dad had been a part of their special occasions and contributed with so much love and affinity. He didn't have any selfish bone in him; he helped and did so much for everyone for all these years only out of care and concern. His actions never reflected any selfish motive because the desire to share and help in him remained the same throughout his life, regardless of whether he had less or more. In a world so selfish and self-obsessed where we mostly help others to get something in return, my dad was definitely different, selfless and giving. Asking for help is human nature but to be forever ready to give certainly doesn't come easy to all, and I'm sure many of whom dad helped but never spoke about, if they are reading this, they would remember him because that's what my dad lived for. While dad was well connected, yet he did not believe in monarchy or dictating terms on people. He believed in equality and earning a position of respect, rather than passing it down as legacy. He always stayed away from organised social groups, clubs and cults.

Not only was dad full of life, but he also led an exemplary life worth emulating. Being extremely hardworking and focused since a very early age made dad what he eventually became as a person. He was a very dedicated and bright student who studied most of his life on government scholarship and earned a lot of medals and recognition for it. He was a self-made businessman. Dad was the only family member who didn't take up a government job like his other siblings and decided to venture on his own, regardless of all the hardships that were expected on this path. He never feared failing and that's what he taught us. He never thought twice before taking risks, and it was this fearless nature and experimental attitude that eventually made him such a successful businessman. He never looked down upon any work; for him no work was small. Life was not always the same for him. He had started from scratch and made the most of every possible opportunity that life gave him. In those days, he did not have any luxury of fancy vehicles or comforts of life, but he never gave up.

In the initial years, when dad had to set up his business without any support system or backup, he had to face a lot of struggle and hardship, but he firmly believed that the only key to success was hard work and complete dedication. It was only because of this passion in him that he became a first-generation entrepreneur in his family in the 1970s under the Delhi State Industrial and Infrastructure Development Corporation (DSIDC) first time entrepreneur scheme, something that he was immensely proud of. After months of hard work and analysis, dad imported heavy-duty fumigation machines that were used to kill mosquitoes on a very large scale, becoming the first Indian to do so. He collaborated with reputed companies from America (Leco) and Germany (Swingfog) and ruled over the Indian market with literally zero competition for years. I clearly remember how proud we felt as kids when we used to share details about his work with others as everyone used to find it so different and interesting. His business got him a lot of fame in India. He also played a vital role during the time when India faced dangerous diseases such as plague and provided a lot of help and support to the Indian government for a very long time. He also maintained beautiful and long-lasting relationships with all the foreign companies and their associates he had collaborated with, and they became an extended family to him over the years. In those initial days, he started with a factory in Wazirpur industrial area; life there wasn't easy and comfortable. Dad used to work very hard and never denied any comforts to his family, even if it meant he could not enjoy them himself. From riding scooters to eventually cruising in luxury cars, from a flat in Ashok Vihar to a bungalow in New Friends Colony, dad had earned every success with his dedication and strong will.

Apart from being hardworking and dedicated, he was also a very intelligent and smart man. He was a walking talking 'Google' and telephone directory. In a time when our lives are completely dependent on technology, dad would remember hundreds of phone numbers by heart and would move around in the city without any Google maps as he knew most of the roads by heart. I remember how I would often call up dad for directions when Google had failed. Today, it feels so sad and depressing that my ever-reliable Google map is gone and I am lost on the road of life not knowing what my ultimate destination would be without his guidance. Dad was extremely knowledgeable and well aware of everything around him. One could get into conversation with him on any topic, be it politics, current affairs or anything in general, he was always updated with the latest trends and events around him. He used to enjoy starting his mornings with not one but several newspapers every day. He never missed an opportunity to gather information through any source possible, except social media. He was not on any social media platforms, yet he was more updated and well-versed than anyone of us!

He was a quick learner and never hesitated to try new things or adapt to changes as and when needed. I remember one day, he suddenly called me up and said he wanted to change his WhatsApp display picture. He wanted to set the latest picture he got clicked at mom's sixtieth birthday party. He took directions from me on how to crop and set the picture and that was the last update he had made to his display picture. Even today that photo remains on his WhatsApp, where he looks so dashing and dapper. And of course, that beautiful smile cannot be missed. Funnily, dad was never able to take screenshots of messages and pictures and would often struggle to understand how I used to do it so quickly. Regardless of how many times I tried teaching him, he just could not, and therefore, he would often send me messages and pictures and ask me to crop them and save them for him.

When I was a kid, he would often scold me for being too addicted Bollywood gossip and reading Delhi Times and HT City for fun. He would often lecture me on improving my general knowledge by reading regular newspapers. That reminds me of something very unique. During the pandemic, dad's most important morning ritual used to be sending E-newspapers to many of his friends and family without fail. He would make sure that everyone received their newspapers to read well in time before starting their day. Even during his last few days, when he was down with COVID, dad continued this ritual until he was hospitalised. My husband, who was one of those few who waited eagerly for that paper every morning and saw it as dad's love and blessing, admits that he still misses the ritual. Perhaps it was God's plan that the first newspaper in hard copy that came to our house during the pandemic was the one that had dad's obituary printed in it. His absence hit us so much harder that day.

We all develop many relationships during our lifetime, but as we reach different stages of life and get busy, we find it easier to leave a few of them behind instead of nurturing them. But my dad was different. Any relationship that he ever made, he tried to maintain it to the best of his ability. He remembered people even if he had met them just once. Keeping in touch with them was something that dad was very particular about. And not just his friends, he would even often check on our friends and keep in touch with them and their families just as he did with his gang. I have been told many times by many of my friends that if dad would ever meet them in a restaurant or market, he would greet them with warmth and affection, and in fact, he would often offer to cover their bills or tell the staff not to take money from them saying he would have done the same if his daughter was in their place. That's how he would make everyone around him feel so special and loved. He always taught us that relationships can never be materialistic, and one should never make them on the basis of background and status. He always made constant effort to make all his old and new friends and family feel special; their positions and job profiles never mattered to dad and he treated them all equally. He often reminded them that they could be out of his sight, but they could never be out of his mind.

"Some people may not do great things, but do small things in great ways."

One of his most popular, favourite and regular rituals was his Diwali gifting ritual. Every year, dad used to get ready for Diwali well in advance and would look forward to personally going and meeting most of his friends over a cup of tea or a glass of drink, without fail. This was the most special time of the year for him to bond with his people and let them know that they were special in his life. I remember he would very religiously make his list every year and try his best not to forget any names. It never mattered to him where his friends were, whether they were working or they were retired; all that mattered was to remind them that they were in dad's thoughts forever. So many of them would actually wait to see him once a year, at least for a fun chat. Some would even compliment dad for his concern for his friends. Whether they were in a great position or not, it never mattered to dad as he used to firmly believe that "people, especially when they feel they are forgotten, need that touch of love and feel that there is still someone who thinks of them without a purpose." I'm sure there would be many who would miss his Diwali wishes and love this year and that Diwali gifting will never be the same.

My dad not only lived like a rock star, but he even looked like one. He loved to dress up and would always carry himself smartly. His famous salt and pepper hair, small build, fitted jeans and his stately Nehru jacket made him always stand out in the crowd. He had a very crisp and smart style of dressing. He always loved to flaunt his amazing collection of pocket squares, which he would happily match with all his Nehru jackets, which he had in all possible colours. Every time I think of him and close my eyes to remember him, his commanding voice, smiling face, his watch and pen in place, those specs on his twinkling eyes, perfectly matched shoes that always made him look so dapper and handsome, come to my mind. In the last few years, dad wasn't in the best of his health due to some liver issues, because of which he had lost tremendous amount of weight, but his enthusiasm and infectious energy remained unmatched and so did his charm! He loved perfumes and would always smell so good. He would often drench himself in the best of the brands, and every time he would pass by, the strong fragrance would fill the air all around. In our early years, we used to live in an apartment complex, and the whole building would know that dad had left for office as the whole staircase would be filled with strong fragrance of the perfumes he wore. Once, one of his aunts (his teacher), complimented dad that a tight hug from him made her smell so good that she would always wait for dad to give her those loving hugs. After losing him, I requested mom to share a few of his clothes with me so that I could sense his strong smell in them and feel close to him once again, not to mention they are now my most prized possessions for life.

Dad wasn't a shopaholic when it came to buying for himself. It was often difficult to buy a gift for him. Once on one of my foreign trips I bought a Burberry scarf for him and had to literally force it on him. Though he was initially angry, but surprisingly, this was the only gift from me that he cherished the most and wore it for most gatherings. In fact, he wore it a lot during his last winter and the scarf still carries his fragrance. Every time I miss dad, I smell the scarf. I never imagined how material things become memories of loved ones and give comfort during difficult times.

I never saw him shopping for himself or going crazy about things like most of us do. But he was always ready to spend on us, first for mom, then for us as kids, and finally, for his grandkids. He definitely had a very good taste and sense of style and it was often noticed by many. He had love for watches as well and his favourite was a Rolex. I saw him wearing it on many occasions and after his passing away, I saw him with that watch on. I hold it so many times now, as if I am holding dad's hand.

Not only did he dress well, but he also liked people around him to dress well too. My mom, a complete contrast, is a simple lady, and I would often see them getting into adorable quarrels about the same. Dad was the one who always shopped for mom, and he would make sure to get the best for her. Once, he went to Chennai on a work trip and returned with not one, but 10 heavy, stunning *Kanjivaram sarees*. Although mom had got very angry on dad then, she still wears them with so much love and pride as his choice was always so good. Similarly, once when he was in Kanpur (mom's maternal home), a city known for leather bags back in the 1980s, he went for a casual stroll and came back with beautiful snake leather bags. Mom told me so many stories about how jealous my *nani* (maternal grandmother) got that evening seeing the bags as my *nana* had never done something like that for her! From gifting beautiful shawls to stunning jewellery, he was mom's biggest Santa Claus. On their twenty-fifth anniversary, he gifted her a beautiful diamonds string as a token of his love for her. Those diamonds were sourced and designed by my father-in-law! My dad wasn't really a romantic, but he was a charmer for sure. Mom and dad would often get into big fights in front of Ashok papa when they visited his showroom for jewellery shopping before my marriage. Mom used to hate shopping and dad used to love it, and he would force mom to buy things for herself. Ashok papa would laugh heartily at such a contrasting couple. No wonder they say opposites attract! Dad made mom's sixtieth birthday celebration in 2019 so memorable, even though mom had resisted the celebration so much. It was his last big get-together with all his near and dear ones. Today, it feels so strange as if he knew what was coming up next. He assumed the role of the perfect host and made sure all our family and friends enjoyed that night and made everyone eat and drink to their heart's content. He never celebrated any of his birthdays and that is something that really hurts me even today. I wonder which perfect celebration he was waiting for all this while, but he always made our days so special with his warmth and generosity. He left making mom's sixtieth birthday so special and memorable for all of us.

Today, his wardrobes filled with clothes look so lifeless and meaningless as if everything inside them have lost the spark and fragrance that was there only because of dad. He used to make the most ordinary thing look so classy and branded with his style and persona. But his personality had two sides, one was living larger than life and the other was simplicity and humility, which he preferred. No matter how grand his persona was and how larger than life he appeared, from the inside he was a very simple man who always remained attached to his humble background. He enjoyed simple food, his favourite being potatoes in any form. I remember during COVID when I would cook for him, every time I asked for his preference he would say any potato dish would do and eat it so happily and with utmost content. But as potatoes have natural sugar, I was asked to avoid it and so I would look for alternatives, and he would get very irritated at that. On the day when he was leaving for hospital and was very unwell and not eating anything, I made his favourite potatoes and paneer dish in red gravy hoping he might eat a bite or two, but the tiffin was left untouched and he left without eating the last meal I had cooked for him.

I never saw dad ever cribbing or making any fuss about food, not even at home or while ordering at restaurants. He was a firm believer in the idea that we eat to live, not live to eat. Food was never his priority; he would be happy and content even if he was served the most basic of dishes like *khichri*. He would eat it with so much happiness. He would get irritated if someone made fuss about food in front of him, but he never tried to control our tastes and food preferences ever. However, his biggest weakness was sweets and was often caught stealing a piece here and there from the sweet box in mom's absence. At weddings, he would be seen relishing rich almond hot milk (kulhad wala badam dhoodh) with so much fondness. While, he never made any fuss about anything related to food, he had a few favorites including India Habitat Centre, Delhi Gymkhana Club and the paan bhandar outside Claridges Hotel. He loved paan! So much so that the famous 'panditji' making paan knew not only him very well, but also his preference for meetha patta, bhuni supari and saada paan. He would get it packed for mom, especially on the days when she would be upset or if dad was running late, this would be his sure shot defense.

He had simple yet strong religious beliefs. He would never miss his regular visits to his favourite Hanuman *Mandir* in New Friends Colony every Tuesday and Bhairon *Mandir* near Pragati Maidan. He was a big follower of *Mata Rani*, too, and *Navratras* were very special to him. Every Navratras he used to make sure that he visited Kalkaji temple to offer his prayers. He respected others religious beliefs and never looked down upon them. As I am an ardent *Guruji* follower, he would quietly attend all *satsangs* at my home with full dedication and even enjoyed the *langar prashad*. Till the very end, his religious beliefs remained very simple and grounded, and he followed them with all his simplicity.

He loved fun movies and hated them if they were very high on emotion. He would say, "We come to watch movies to unwind ourselves and relax so what's the point watching movies that send us back home with tears or a heavy heart." He would laugh like a kid at movies such as *Golmaal* and *House Full*, basically any movie where there was only fun and no tension. One of his all-time favourite movies was *Lamhe* and his favourite song, "*Dikhai diye yu ki bekhud kiya*" which he would often be caught humming, was from an old movie *Bazaar*. Even when it came to his choice of songs and movies, he always preferred something simple and relatable. He would often joke with us that our generation was full of drama.

This was my simple yet special dad. He was so unique. Be it his dressing style or his attitude, everything about him was grand and larger than life. No wonder his fan following is so vast and extends across different generations and even different counties and continents. He was one of the most loyal friends one could ever have. He was someone who would stand beside you when others had left, extend a helping hand when others didn't, without making it obvious. Often, he would help people financially, without letting his immediate family know about it. Much of it came to light after he had left. He would sign cheques to people in need and many of them never even returned the money. But none of that ever stopped dad from doing the good that he enjoyed doing. For dad showing involvement meant just being around and supporting to the best of his capacity, even if it meant just dropping a message to show he was always around when needed or showing that the other person was forever in his thoughts. Help not only meant monetary assistance for him, it was also pure and selfless concern.

Just the other day an officer posted outside Delhi called up to tell my mom that dad was so instrumental in shaping his son's future and career — dad had sponsored the kid's first computer when he needed it the most. He would find friends in different groups of people and age groups and would beautifully and effortlessly maintain the relationship, treating them all as a part of his life. Be it his school or college groups, his favourite walking gang of New Friends Colony or his famous 'Darbar' at the Lodhi Hotel, he would make time for all of them. Sometimes, I wonder how dad managed it all and that too so well; he was truly a rock star!

There are many who were a part of these various groups, and today, they often share stories about how that one smile from dad would make everything fall into place. Be it planning any reunion or the famous Sunday chai get-together in the colony, where friends recall him being a regular and punctual walker who would often pass them in the morning with that one warm smile, or his famous table at the Lodhi Hotel where so many would join him for a cup of coffee and chat, the list remains endless! Dad wore many hats, yet he never complained or ever judged anyone. He trusted people with complete acceptance too often and quickly without doubts. He was never a part of any gossip group and remained as neutral as he could in most of his relationships. He was forever available for family and even their friends as well as for friends and their families. He always believed life was all about taking risks and living in the moment and that's what he did until his last breath. For the person he was, dad shall be remembered everyday but especially in moments of happiness and success. I will always remember that he was in some way, big or small, behind those memorable moments. His magnanimity ensured that he touched the lives of innumerable people with such moments, leaving behind memories that would last forever.

'Do things for people not because of who they are or what they do in return but because of who you are'

Dad in younger days

5

Dad's Endless Love for His *Alma Mater*

Most of us love our *alma mater*, but there are very few people, the special ones, who are loved back in return. It is totally impossible to visualise dad without his educational institutions, to which he remained faithful and attached till his very last breath. The pride that dad had for his college and school was unmatchable. Even years after passing out, we all remember our school and college very fondly, but dad was among those who was remembered by the institutions he had studied in for the exceptional work and commitment he had shown in his lifetime. This was one of those special associations in his life that gave him a lot of happiness and pride. Just the mention of his *alma mater* would light up his eyes and bring a smile to his face. A major part of his life revolved around his school and college and the efforts that he would put into helping these institutions when needed. He also tried his best to connect with as many fellow students as he could manage to do. He was instrumental in organising numerous reunions and get-togethers that would, eventually, help in bringing back so many batchmates in contact with each other. The selfless person that he was, he never hesitated to connect with people and help them. Till his last breath, he remained a proud blue-blooded Modernite and a proud Stephanian.

Dad joined school in 1957 as a resident student. He managed most of his schooling as a scholarship holder and was an extremely bright and a hardworking student. Not only did he excel in studies, he was also a hockey player, an athlete and a national-level debater. He participated in various plays and never backed out from any responsibilities and duties. He won the hearts of his fellow batchmates and teachers with his helpful nature and warm smile. No wonder many of his classmates share stories about his popularity as a boarding house prefect, keeping everybody happy and content. He was successful in creating a healthy balance between being with the most studious and the most notorious students without ever getting into any challenging situation. He was everyone's favourite and that is the reason so many of them miss him so much today.

With most of them, he created a lasting and meaningful bond and kept in touch with them even after years of passing out from school. During his school days, he once participated in a relief fund program and was recognised by the school for selling the maximum number of tickets that too by cycling non-stop and covering the maximum number of nearby colonies and areas and raising the highest amount, for which he was even awarded by Pandit Nehru who was the chief guest at the school's founder's day celebration. He passed out from school in 1970 and the year 2020 marked the golden jubilee celebration of his batch. The excitement of this celebration was visible in his eyes as he was involved with the organising committee for this celebration. But as God had planned, this much-awaited celebration never happened because of the pandemic, which made him so upset. This also coincided with the 100 years celebration of the school, which each one of us was looking forward to. Unfortunately, dad was not destined to be a part of this grand celebration.

After his demise, his batchmates from all over the world spoke so fondly of the beautiful memories dad had made with them while organising the 50 year reunion. They shared their feelings though a beautiful farewell meeting they all organized on zoom and got together from all parts of the world for their most loved friend Suresh! They all said how important a role he had played in bringing all of them together once again after so long. We all take from school in many ways as it lays the foundation of our upbringing, but there are very few people like dad who believed in giving back much more to his institutions in return for what he had received. His regular involvement in various activities and groups at his school was his way of giving back to the school in the best way possible, be it starting awards and sponsorships in his father's memory and helping many students like him to grow or by funding various school projects and events every time he was asked to. He always treated his *alma mater* as his extended family, about which he always felt so strongly and held so close to his heart. I remember that even as his daughter, I had no idea how much he had contributed and he never spoke about it openly. Once on the school's founder's day celebration, in which my daughter had participated in a play, I was taken by surprise when my grandfather's name was announced during the awards ceremony, and there were not one but four awards in his memory started by dad for the best students of class 6, 7, 8 and 9. As the excitement got so visible on my face, my daughter happily announced that the awards were named after her great-grandfather and that the initiative was taken by her *nanu*. The rest of the evening we had parents requesting us jokingly to recommend their child's name for the award next year; the whole experience left me feeling so proud of my Dad. Later in the evening when I shared it with dad, he just smiled and said that every year the school would invite him and request to be seated in the VIP area and attend the ceremony and he would miss it as he didn't want any attention because he solely did it for the love of his school and, most importantly, in the memory of his beloved father. He also joked with me that now that Manya was in school, the following year he should proudly sit in that VIP section and enjoy the evening watching her perform on the stage from a closer distance. I had wished that the next year I would make sure I would attend it with dad and enjoy, but it remained an unfulfilled wish.

Unlike many of us who get busy in their usual life after passing out from school, dad not only stayed in touch with many of his friends, but he also took many initiatives to keep in touch with his school and teachers, extending help for dinners, tournaments and other events organised at the school. His association went a long way, and one such association that he had made with his favourite Hindi teacher Mr. Chaturvedi comes to mind. Not only did dad stay in touch with him and his family after passing out from school, but he also invited his teacher to join his business after retirement from school. Mr. Chaturvedi worked with dad as long as he was alive, with full respect and honour. In fact, many of dad's batchmates would get a big surprise seeing Mr. Chaturvedi in dad's office when they visited dad from other cities and would feel touched to see dad's beautiful gesture of continuing his faith in the ideology of *Gurudakshina* (being grateful to your teachers for the education they have given you and giving back to them as a mark of your respect). Dad even acted as the secretary of the old students association and was actively involved as an executive committee member of MSOSA (Modern School Old Students Association) till he lived. He made me join the MSOSA last year as a member and was so excited about it that we would get to attend meetings together now. Unfortunately, it could not happen due to COVID. Dad was the convener of the 50 year celebration event and so he asked me to volunteer but the event was cancelled due to the onset of the second wave. In fact, just a few days before getting admitted to the hospital, he had committed to donate money for the *guru pranam* initiative to help the retired teachers of his school. Even though by that time he was COVID-positive and unwell, his attachment to his *alma mater* remained unaffected and unchanged till the very end.

He had a lot of affection for his school friends, irrespective of the batch or age. All it mattered was that they went to the same school. He would find a Modernite in any part of the world; be it on a flight or country or street, just meeting them would light up his eyes and it was enough to create a bond! In fact, he would often get into arguments if anyone ever said anything wrong about his school. He always held his school in high regard and took so much pride that it was tough to match his love towards the institution. I once joked with him that I would prefer sending my daughter to a world school as it had better facilities. One cannot even begin to imagine the long lecture I got from him that day. He told me Modern School had a legacy that not many institutions could even think to ever match, and that I should look to have a street-smart child instead of one dependent on the luxuries of life, which one can still have after school. The debater in him would always win any argument that revolved around his school. He got so many of his family kids and friends' children admitted in the school for the same belief in the legacy of Modern School. Dad always happily accompanied us to all school events, leaving mom behind as he did not want to miss any opportunity to go back to his school.

After passing out from school, he joined the prestigious St. Stephen's College in Delhi University as an economics honours student in 1971. He carried over the same enthusiasm and commitment from school to his college and his college friends. Till the end, he never missed any of his yearly college Sunday lunches in the college mess. I had the honour of attending one of these lunches with him as we both went to the same college. For the first time, I witnessed a child-like enthusiasm in dad when I saw him jumping from one table to another in the college mess, meeting and enjoying with his friends. That excitement in his eyes was unexplainable and unbeatable. This was instrumental in creating a much-talked-about and interesting lunch group with fellow Stephanians, where he himself hosted some amazing lunches with his friends, and for that he will be remembered for a long time. Many of his friends spoke about those lunches after he left. They even went on to say that they would certainly miss attending these lunches now that "there will be no Suresh bhai to give any early morning reminders for the college lunches now." A lot of times dad would reach even before the actual host and welcome everyone at the gate himself. Surprisingly, even I had asked him to take me along on many occasions as it had grown into a popular and prestigious group of Stephanians, but dad being an honest man clearly told me to earn my entry and not ask for his help! He wouldn't even get me entry to lunches that he hosted himself.

He would often flaunt the amazing collection of his school and college memorabilia. He collected many of them, including pens, mugs, wall clocks, key chains and many more, with a lot of happiness and pride. Not to forget the biggest proof of his loyalty for his institutions: he made sure that both his children joined the same school and college as he did and carry the legacy forward. Dad literally danced in the college corridor the day I cleared the college admissions. I had never seen him so happy. It filled him with so much pride that I thanked God that I could do at least this little thing for someone like him. He was also instrumental in getting all his grandchildren enrolled in Modern School and was over the moon seeing the third generation follow his footsteps. I always wanted a three-generation photo with dad in front of the beautiful and grand Modern School building when it was beautifully decorated to celebrate the golden jubilee, but could not because of the pandemic. My wish will now forever remain unfulfilled. His dream to see his granddaughter Manya also join the same college was also left unfulfilled. We plan so many things about our future, but we fail to remember the biggest fact of life that what's already written in our destiny can never be changed or altered, and what wins eventually is only the Divine will. It gives me so much pain that so many of our wishes were left incomplete as it all happened just so suddenly.

After Stephen's, dad joined the Faculty of Management Studies (FMS) for his MBA. Needless to say, he gave back to the institute too, and for years, helped in providing scholarships to many students and supported them wholeheartedly. Every year, he actively participated in organising the annual dinner, for which he would get gold medals made for the scholars, and contributed in whatever way he could. For the endless support that he gave to the institution, in the year 2020, he was elected as the president of the FMS' old student fraternity and was recognised for the amazing and selfless work he had done for so many years. This election as the president had brought dad a lot of joy; however, he did not know he would not be able to complete his tenure. But it goes without saying that as long as he lived, he not only stayed connected to his *alma mater* in his best capacity but also contributed in their growth in every way possible.

Dad was the best of friends anyone could ever wish for. He had the knack of making people feel special and wanted. His humble nature and warmth reflected in each and every friendship he had ever had. He always treated his friends as his extended family, and when opportunity would arrive, he would make sure to make them feel the same. He stood by them in tough and good times, rejoiced in their victories and always lent his shoulder to cry on when they were sad. Dad was always the first one to reach and help. Unlike many others in today's world, dad never sang praises of his deeds. When dad would be around, no one ever needed to spend. He would always come forward and be the first one to pay when in a group, always ready with his trademark wallet. He would push his friends aside when the time came to pay. He simply wouldn't have it. He would not do it to gain any recognition as I truly believe you can do such things once in a while to attract attention, but if one is always doing it repeatedly, it's surely an example of their giving and helping nature.

Many of dad's outstation friends spoke about how, for a long time, dad had remained their only point contact every time they visited Delhi. He was their home away from home. Dad was always just a call away. From arranging quick reunions, airport pick-ups to shopping trips, he would organise everything. He would even get them connected to more of his friends around. He would never forget to treat them to one of his few favourite places, such as his all-time favourite Oriental Octopus at the India Habitat Centre and the famous Lodhi Hotel coffee area next to the pool, so that they would leave Delhi with loads of beautiful memories. Even today, when we hear about their Delhi trips, I wonder how dad always found so much time to be with all of them. He was never too busy for any of his dear friends, and welcomed them with open heart and arms. People move on and get busy with lives and work, but I am sure that for many of his close friends, Delhi trips will never be the same again as there will be no Suresh Bhai to welcome them with the same warmth and a big cheerful smile.

The amazing networker that dad was, no one could ever beat him at that! I still wonder how he managed such a vast network of friends so effortlessly. Maybe he was a collector of diverse and interesting company. His memory was so sharp that no one could ever beat him at that. One only had to take a name and dad would know everything about that person, his education, family background and work experience. No wonder why most of his friends considered dad a walking encyclopaedia. He had knowledge of everything, and hence, for him connecting with people and making things work was always so natural and quick. Just the other day, one of his friends had mentioned that the aura that dad had was unmatched. The moment he would walk into a room, he would change the whole vibe and everything would just fall into place. On one such occasion dad had accompanied a friend to one of the ministry offices to get an important work done that was badly needed to help that friend. Upon reaching there, the atmosphere got very tensed and the job didn't seem to head in the positive direction. Just then, dad started the conversation with the officer and soon they realised they had many old friends and batchmates in common, and as the conversation progressed dad not only got his friends work done, he even managed to add that strict officer as a new friend in this list and they continued to keep in touch till the very end. He would make heads turn and win over everyone with his one killer smile. He always loved entertaining people with big or small gatherings; the parties he hosted were full of life and heart. As a matter of fact, those who experienced his big heart would know what it meant to be close to him. Unlike many, he would never bother about expenditures made to entertain his loved ones. No amount of bill ever mattered until he had made sure everyone was well looked after. He hosted these gatherings at the best venue, offered the best alcohol and made sure all his guests ate well and enjoyed. Before he left, dad gave a wonderful gift of true friendship to all his friends, something that they would miss the most as it would definitely be hard to find a friend like him in this lifetime. As one of his dear friends summed it up for him, "*sabhi ka tha tu sabhi the tere* (he belonged to everyone and everyone belonged to him)." He held every relationship so close to his heart till the very end.

Although since 2019, dad was not in the best of his health, his life went on as smooth as it could for someone like him. However, he had become weak from the inside, but for the world outside, he was always strong, smiling and ready to help anyone, anytime, anywhere. Nothing on that front ever changed, even during his worst days. His love towards people remained unaffected despite what he had to go through mentally and physically. He lived life cheerfully and taught others what it meant to live life king size. He never looked back at anything — person or decision — with regrets. His zeal for life was contagious. Whoever came to him for help never left empty-handed. As many fellow Modernites and Stephanians would attest, his radiant ebullient life truly deserves to be beautifully remembered as one lived with contentment, patience and inner strength. People might have different perspectives about him, but the most common of all has always remained unchanged — he was foremost a friend's true friend as I have already said, '*yaaron ka yaar.*' He was someone who never announced his entry into anyone's life, but once he had entered, he was there to stay by their side through all the ups and downs of life. That was the most beautiful thing about him. He was always thoughtful and would check on his friends every once in a while and let them know he was always there for them whenever needed. He was always the first one to make an effort to keep in touch with everyone.

"Some people love you; some people love to be around you; some love what you can do for them. All you need to do is understand the difference well."

SURESH GUPTA

Suresh Gupta was the Boarding House prefect. Good in studies, he was equally good at elocution. He was awarded the elocution prize on the Founder's day. A good sportsman, Suresh was a member of the school ruggertouch team. Active at dramatics he acted in many a House Play.

Suresh strived hard to maintain a reasonable standard of discipline in the Boarding House. He worked hard for the Boarding House Fete, held in aid of the Lepers' Relief Fund for which he won a special prize on the Founder's day.

Dad during his school days

Dad with smt. Indira Gandhi (former prime minister of India) during his school's founders day

Modern School Old Students' Association
Executive Committee 2018-2020

Dad as an executive committee member of MSOSA

Dad giving awards and scholarships in his late father's memory at FMS

Haripat Rai Memorial Gold Medal being awarded.

Dad with St. Stephens college's principal Dr Wilson and other college friends

Dad with some of his favorite college friends

Dad with 1970 batch per reunion get together

6

And COVID Hits Us Bad

Some battles are lost even before they are fought!

It was that time of the year once again, yet it was so different this time. One could feel the nip in the air, that slight chilly weather, festivities all around. It is Diwali time — Diwali 2021. This festival is the hardest to get through without a loved one as you feel so alone and incomplete, with a host of emotions clubbed together. It's our first Diwali without dad and so it doesn't feel like a festival anymore. Everyone seems to be happy, celebrating, excited and full of energy, unlike us who would have to deal with the emptiness in our life left by the departure of an irreplaceable family member. As my car passes through the colony gate, I see houses lit with bright yellow lights, while some houses are still engulfed in darkness, mourning the loss of a loved one to the pandemic. Celebrations are in full swing but the hollowness in my heart doesn't seem to settle. No matter how hard I try not to think about it, I can't help seeing people in so much excitement this year, going out to endless parties and celebrations as if there is no tomorrow, unaware of what those families would be feeling or going through after a personal loss this year. I guess it is so true that no one ever feels the pain until people lose their very own, yet it's always good to be a little compassionate towards others. Time doesn't wait for anyone and life moves on for most. For most life seems to be back to normal, parties travelling, holiday shopping and any celebrations that makes then happy to be back with a bang! Even though it's been almost six months since we lost dad, it seems as if it all just happened yesterday. God! Six months already and this pain just doesn't seem to go, no matter how hard I try. Festivals like this make it even more difficult to deal with the pain. The Diwali madness was something I used to wait for all year round, but suddenly, I don't fit in those selfie pics with my friends anymore; it was something I was known for in every party I went to. How can so much change in your life and that too so soon? It was just yesterday when this deadly disease COVID had knocked at our doors and the nightmare began!

Just in a span of two weeks, it was all over. Time slipped out of my hand just as sand spills out of a closed fist. When Delhi was facing the deadly second wave in mid-April, it all felt so scary as people had not even recovered completely from the shock of the first wave in March 2020. This felt even worse! The first lockdown left people focusing more on priorities, enjoying home-cooked food, having fun on house party app and video calls, standing in grocery lines for hours and getting familiar for the first time with a completely new set of terminologies such as isolation, quarantine, jab and many more. The first wave was all about being safe and protected. Even during that time, I saw my parents going through so much stress for staying safe and taking precaution should the disease ever knock on their door! I used to often tell them to stay positive and have faith that this too shall pass, but I never knew it would actually hit us so bad. Just as after the first wave had settled and life seemed to have come back a bit on track, I, who had waited to see my own parents for months during the first wave, was so relieved that I could at least spend some time with them. Suddenly, life had looked so much more beautiful. From January 2021 to April 2021, god gave me so many opportunities to spend time with dad. I finally got to spend time with my parents, especially dad. I should say it was God's way to keep me close to him as he knew what was coming up next. Unlike so many years that had gone by, this year started on an exceptionally beautiful note. I spent my first day of new year with dad and the rest of the family; it was just so blissful. I even visited my *Guruji's mandir* on 1 January to offer my prayers, not knowing that *Guruji* had called me so far to give me courage to stay strong for the rest of the year. I still remember it was 24 April early morning, mom and my brother were showing signs of fever and were in self-isolation. My phone rang and it was mom on the other side, worried and tensed. As she spoke, I somehow felt the inevitable was coming true. They all had been afraid that COVID would hit my maternal house ever since the first wave. That fear had taken over most of them completely already.

Mom told me that my brother was unwell and was being rushed to the hospital. I feared for my brother's health and was very tensed and worried, but I was hoping dad wasn't going with him to the hospital as just a day before a friend had called and said that things were extremely bad in Delhi and hospitals had become the biggest hub of infection and just no one at all should go there. As soon as I said this to my mom, she scolded me badly and said dad wouldn't listen. He was determined to go as he was the one coordinating the hospital admissions and everything that was needed. I wanted to keep dad safe so I requested Manish to accompany him. I won't lie but as a wife and daughter, it was a tough decision to make as Manish had gone through a bad COVID infection during the first wave and was still recovering. I wanted him to be safe as well, but having no choice, I sent him with a heavy heart to drive dad down to the hospital after my brother's car.

After my brother was admitted, mom's health started deteriorating. Tension and pressure began to build, and on 27 April, dad called and told me that mom needed hospitalisation too as her condition wasn't getting stable at home at all. I just could not believe how one by one my family was getting caught in the clutches of the pandemic that too when they had for almost a year taken every possible precaution. They had not ventured out at all and were vaccinated too. I had hardly met my parents in 2020, as they feared I could be a carrier of infection. They had no part-time staff, no drivers were allowed, and they were literally cut off from the world. Dad, in fact, was most badly affected due to this new normal; being so social and outgoing, it was a very rough year for him. He had not seen and met his friends and family for a really long time and was waiting anxiously for things to go back to the way they were before the pandemic. Today, it feels so sad to think that he didn't even get the chance to meet the people he really wanted to for the last time at least. Dad badly missed his lunches at Lodhi, morning walks with the New Friends Colony gang, family reunions, his college monthly lunches and connecting with his loved ones. After we lost dad, mom told me that in the last few months, especially after dad had heard that the second wave was around the corner, he had started to lose all hopes and had begun to feel extremely depressed as the pandemic seemed never-ending to him. It felt so sad that he was actually trapped in a long and lonely period of isolation. Before he could see the pandemic restrictions eased, he was unfortunately gone. It makes me think and feel sorry that like my dad there were so many who had lost the battle to loneliness before they did to COVID. Now when I see life going back to normal and people rejoicing for making it through the second wave (some even joking about how it was all a facade and nothing was serious), my heart feels so sad and gets filled with anger at these people who would never understand the pain that many families like us experienced. We lost this battle so bad that we shall never be able to celebrate this victory, unlike others who seem so unaffected by this tragedy.

As we prepared to admit mom in the hospital, another horror began. The national capital had exhausted all its resources; RTPCR was taking 72 hours, CT scans had a one-week waiting time, ambulances were being bribed to carry patients and getting hospital admissions was the biggest nightmare. Amidst so much madness and chaos, my very dear school friend, whose family headed one of the biggest hospital chains in Delhi at that time, came to my rescue. It was very odd because despite being friends since the age of four years, we had grown a bit distant as we lived in different cities. We were unable to connect often as we had to manage our responsibilities as a wife and a mother. It was tough to suddenly call her up and ask for help, a habit that never came naturally to me and always made me very uncomfortable. I am sure it was another trait passed down by dad, who always taught us as kids to be a giver and not someone who is always seeking help. I always saw dad helping people and never asking for anything in return, and most importantly, never make friends to fulfil a purpose. He taught us to be friends with those who touch our soul and make us feel wanted and loved, so it was somehow very tough for me to suddenly, for the first time in my life, ask for favours from a friend like that. And as God had wanted, unfortunately, this series of favours was endless this time, starting from the first request of arranging a hospital bed to finally asking for arranging a cremation spot at the crematorium. It all happened so fast that it's tough to swallow it even today.

Having said that, I will forever be grateful to my friend and her husband for being there at the time when we were most vulnerable. She remained my pillar of support and strength in the most stressful phase of my life.

As I managed to arrange a bed in the hospital for mom with my friend's help and prepared to take her with me, I never knew that the journey from there would be so tough. Even while being admitted, mom was only concerned about dad as she had never left him alone before. Even in the past, when she would fall ill or get hospitalised, dad would book the best suite in the hospital and shift with her. So, this time it was definitely tough for both of them. As mom was leaving for the hospital, looking so weak and drained, dad came out in the balcony to see her off and waved her a loving goodbye. She never knew it would be her last meeting with dad in this lifetime. I finally managed to admit her in the hospital in the same room as my brother. I returned home with a bit of relief as now it was only dad who had to be taken care of. Once mom got settled in the hospital, I requested dad to get tested for COVID so that I could enter the house and look after him. After a lot of resistance, he agreed and we got his RTPCR done that day itself. Just as I was preparing to hold the fort strongly and manage everything in mom's absence, in came the biggest shock — dad had tested positive too. It felt like my biggest fear was coming true. It was not something that was totally unexpected as dad had come into close contact with mom and the rest of the family, but I was surely praying it not to come true, no matter what. I now saw my whole family being badly getting trapped in the web of the pandemic.

The task of breaking the news to dad seemed impossible to me. He had always been very sensitive and afraid of medical treatments and any kind of illness. He always ran away from needles and tests. Moreover, it was scarier as dad had a history of weak liver and had been on a long treatment for the same, surprisingly the doctor who was treating dad for his liver issue from a renowned liver speciality hospital, was also not staying in touch or attending to his patients due to the onset of the first wave of the pandemic. Unfortunately, by the time we realised, dad had already stopped most of his liver medications as the doctor was not replying to the messages or ready to assist him for the same as his condition was to meet the patients physically in a crowded hospital. It was not possible for dad to go in the prevailing circumstances. So internally, he was very weak and fragile. I knew this and that's why finding out that dad was COVID-positive scared me. It was impossible to pass the night when his report came on 29 April, and I waited for morning to break the news to him. As I told him, there was complete silence on the phone on the other side. I, as his daughter, could sense the fear building up in his breath. Today, I feel like dad had actually given up that very day. What happened after that was a manifestation of the belief that most of the people hold for COVID. It was the fear of not being able to survive. Those days were marked by the fear of death, inability to arrange resources when needed and a constant struggle for survival. I felt it was important to remain positive and involve oneself more and more in chanting and praying so we could evoke a higher power for our safety and protection, but people were instead busy hoarding medicines, injections, cylinders and concentrators. Ideally, if we would have remained together and strong mentally, many would not have lost this battle the way they all did, just like my own father.

My heart was sinking as I knew deep inside that he was very scared and he was all alone for the first time ever. By now even the rest of the family (daughter-in-law and kids) had quarantined themselves on a separate floor for their safety and dad was all alone. No matter how hard my husband and I tried, dad refused to let us in the house to take care of him. As I had already handled Manish's health and recovery during the first wave, I had some idea and I felt competent enough to look after dad, but he just refused to come to my house and neither did he let me inside his floor. Finally, Manish and I decided to take care of him from a distance as much as we could, from arranging meals, to never-ending video calls with doctors, series of tests and scans and endless trips to pharmacies. It all looked so tough and crazy; it was a testing time. With hardly any staff due to the lockdown and the fear of getting infected, it was a path to be walked alone. Moreover, having no clue where we were heading, it just felt so scary and lonely. I was coordinating with the hospital for my brother and mother's well-being and looking after dad, who from being asymptomatic in the first few days had started to develop the symptoms slowly. At times, I just felt like pinching myself hard to wake up from this nightmare that I was being made to go through. For years, I had lived as a married daughter, who would occasionally visit her parents and keep in touch. After being married for 15 years, our lifestyles were different and so much had changed over the years. Suddenly, to be a part of their lives once again and that too without a choice was tough. It was like being thrown into a situation completely unaware and unprepared, and on top of it all, a very strong fear of losing dad made this even more difficult to handle. Then began the week-long ordeal of running from pillar to post, looking for oxygen cylinders, concentrators and steroids, followed by crazy, sleepless nights when Manish and I waited to see dad active on WhatsApp as an assurance of him being fine and safe. I do feel that although we felt so alone, there were so many like us at that time going through a similar situation, some perhaps even worse. Updates of people losing lives everywhere; new-born kids being orphaned and requests for adoption; families losing their only son, their only bread earner to this disease; or helpless people struggling badly to get hospital beds and ultimately dying in cars unable to get the treatment on time; more than two members dying of COVID in one family alone; and people actually fighting to get crematorium spots or place to burn their loved ones; it was all just so heart-breaking and unimaginable to witness.

Meanwhile, in the middle of all this, dad held a strong front, at least for us so that we didn't get scared. He attended the never-ending calls that poured in to ask about mom's and brother's well-being. Often, I could sense the fear of losing them in our conversations. He just wanted them to be back home soon and be with them like old times. He was still keeping in constant touch with all his friends and family as much as he could. During this time, dad was losing a lot of his acquaintances too. No matter how hard I tried hiding all messages and posts from him, he would know and was badly getting affected as he saw the fear realising each day.

I remember calling him only to find him dull and upset. When I inquired, he told me he had lost a dear friend to COVID who was younger to him. He regretted the fact that the pandemic had turned all money and contacts virtually ineffective. All one needed now was prayers and miracles. Even during such stressful times, dad had not lost his sharpness and thoughtfulness. When mom needed an immediate delivery of an in-demand steroid, I decided to arrange it at any cost from the black market. Dad being his usual self said that it wasn't the right way to do it at all and even opposed my decision even during such challenging times when most people were just giving up. He said that we should stay calm and patient and let the hospital arrange it for he feared that the one available in the market might not be authentic and hospital might not agree to use it either. Dad being so proactive even at such a time was just so commendable. He was always a man of honour, only willing to do things the right way. He held that belief strongly till the end.

Meanwhile, there was something different about those few days with him alone. He lovingly ate the food I sent for him for the first time ever since I got married. Before this, he had never agreed to come over and have a meal at my place. In fact, just at that time my cook had left as she feared for her safety too in this crazy situation, seeing the whole family slowly getting affected. I was left to do the cooking all by myself. Although I wasn't a good cook, I cooked for him under a lot of fear and stress. Dad called me later and told me that he had loved the food I made and that it tasted better than what the cook used to make. His words left me happy and emotional. We kept in touch through non-stop calls and messages and spoke about a variety of things, from mom to movies, friends and politics and much more. After a long time, I had the opportunity to connect with dad once again and take care of him as a mother, something that I had never imagined I would do. Surprisingly, it was a beautiful time to bond in the middle of so much chaos and tension. There were days I would break down under pressure and feel bad for being helpless and alone, but then dad would send me a message saying he was proud of me and it would lift me up all over again and give me so much strength, even in the most critical situation. It was surely OUR time! This time gave me the most special memories that are only and only mine, and I shall cherish them with a smile and silent tears for the rest of my life.

All this while, dad didn't even share the news of him being COVID-positive with anyone as he didn't want to divert attention towards himself; he wanted everyone to pray for the speedy recovery of the rest of the family as soon as possible. All he wanted was for them to be back home so he could see them safe and fine, maybe for one last time, a wish that could not be fulfilled, regardless of how hard we tried. The selfless human that he was, he didn't even give his loved ones enough time and opportunity to pray for his recovery as he was still so concerned for the rest of the family.

Eventually, my worst fear began to come true and dad started showing more symptoms. I was advised by dad's dear school friend who is a practicing general physician from Defence Colony, to hospitalise him due to his age and He continuously guided me and suggested the right treatment for dad. So at first I decided to connect with the same liver specialist to take opinion on dad's health as I thought he knew dad's medical history well to guide us in the right direction. Just to get through to him for one appointment became a nightmare which I somehow managed through a friend's help. But as I should have guessed, he came across as least concerned and helpful in the hour of crisis even though it took us two sleepless nights to get the medical synopsis ready but eventually no advice from his side helped or gave any relief. I had then connected with a very famous doctor of a top Delhi hospital for dad's consultation and had even requested him to not share any stressful news when dad was on the call, but he turned out to be extremely rude and tough and didn't speak well to dad at all. The irony was that he was from the same school. Even in such tensed situation, dad very warmly told him the same and even complimented him on the great job he was doing as a successful doctor, but instead of reciprocating to dad's warmth with kindness, he behaved in a very cold manner, giving dad the first big blow of terror that I was trying to keep him away from all this while. For the first time, he felt things were no more in control and were not heading in a positive direction; for the first time, my dad feared death!

As soon as that call got over and I told dad about the hospitalisation, the first thing he said was, "Don't send me to the hospital, Divya. I'll never come back."

Even today, these words haunt me. When he said this, I just went numb and decided not to push him as that would have affected his health more. I understood that doctors had to go through a lot during the pandemic, but I felt such deep anger at that doctor at that time. Had he been able to handle the situation a little better and not behaved the way he did, my dad would have never lost hope and courage. I struggled to arrange a home ICU for him, but it seemed so impossible at that time. So, I decided to get him a 24-hour attendant as I just could not leave him alone at night unattended. It was a difficult task to look for one in those challenging days, but I did finally manage to get one for dad. By now, one of my cousins had also shifted in with dad to look after him. It did bring temporary relief to dad as he was a bit happy to have someone around. By then, my dad had become lonely and sad. On the seventh day of COVID, I was up all night and was trying to be in touch with the attendant. But when he did not pick my calls, I got alarmed, and then, he informed me that at 3 am for the first time dad's oxygen had dropped. An oxygen concentrator was being used, and by then, he had become restless, uncomfortable and unwell. I immediately decided it was time to go to the hospital no matter what. I did not want to waste even a day as we had waited enough already. Surprisingly, even during such a crazy time, dad wanted family's approval to make any decisions, which led to delay in taking so many important decisions, but finally we all reached the same conclusion.

That very morning, I requested my friend again for another bed and this time for dad, the most important one in my life. No matter how hard I tried, I just could not explain my friend what it would mean for me to lose him and how badly I wanted him to get well. As a daughter and friend, she did try her best to help me in whatever capacity she could, but unfortunately, could not get the hospital of our choice! Dad wanted to go to the same hospital where the rest of the family was admitted and wanted to be with them. We tried our best, but we just could not manage, given the situation. We were left with no choice as dad totally refused to go anywhere else. It fell upon me to convince him. Manish told me it was time we met dad in person and convince him. I had not seen dad for so many days and was unsure if I was ready to do so, but Manish insisted. As I prepared myself to finally enter the house to meet dad, it gave me goosebumps. It was a feeling that I still cannot put in words. Why did Manish say it was time to meet him? I got so mad at him that day, but I finally decided to go and meet him.

As I entered the house, it looked so incomplete without mom for the first time. The house was in a mess, and there was my dad, a once so cheerful and dashing man, but today, he looked so weak, unwell and scared lying in bed. My heart sank seeing him in that condition. However, his eyes began to glow as soon as he saw me. After all, I was the first family member he had seen after so many days and at a time when he needed it the most. I must add that COVID killed as many people with loneliness, which left them so fearful and scared, as it did with infection. When one falls sick, it is the love of the closest ones that helps one to recover and bounce back, but this disease had left everyone so helpless and paranoid that the journey ahead seemed totally impossible. Dad was no exception. He had always stood by those in need, helping everyone in his best capacity, but today, he was all alone and weak, all because of the pandemic. He had seen so much in life and had experienced all the bitter and sweet moments that life gave him, yet he was taken aback upon seeing what the pandemic had done to the world. In his last days, he kept wondering about what had suddenly happened and whether things would ever be normal again. These thoughts left him so confused and lost.

As I stood outside his room, he told me to come inside. Manish had told me not to enter the room because by now dad had begun showing all the symptoms of COVID, but as soon as dad asked me to come, the daughter in me could not refuse and I went inside. I sat down on a nearby chair and kept looking at him. My dad, once so energetic and full of life, looked so pale and weak. He was coughing badly and was so uncomfortable. By now his appetite had also drastically reduced and he seemed to have lost more weight than before. It gave me so much pain to see him like that, but I held myself strong in front of him. This was in contrast to my actual situation at home, where I was breaking down every few hours due to the immense pressure and tension. I explained to him that it was now time to go to the hospital and told him he was my hero and he could not loose, no matter what. I told him there were so many people struggling for hospital beds and we were fortunate enough to get one and we could not leave this opportunity even for a day. I told him to trust me, which he eventually did; for that, I would always feel guilty as I could not win over his trust sooner.

Suddenly, he asked me if I could immediately arrange five to six good-quality oxygen concentrators to gift to a few of his friends. For a moment, I paused. To be honest, I got a bit irritated. How could he think about gifting oxygen concentrators in the middle of so much tension? But, dad being dad, said we never know whose blessings would work, so we should keep helping. I promised him that if he got well soon, I would immediately do what he wanted as during that time arranging good-quality concentrators was just impossible. After I finally convinced him, I told him to get ready and I started preparing to go back to make all the arrangements. Just then, one of the staff called and told dad that Manish had been waiting in the car downstairs for quite some time. My lovable dad scolded me for making him sit in the car in the summer heat, and that I should leave immediately. As I got up, I told dad I was dying to hug him tight and that I felt so helpless for not being able to do so. All he did was smile. When I came back home, the attendant called me up and told me that right after our meeting, dad's oxygen level had increased and he was a little better. The news made me happy, but today, when I think of it, I feel I should have visited him every day when he was alone. Perhaps I could have given him some happiness and strength to fight the disease back.

Finally, it was time to leave for the hospital. On 7 May, as the ambulance arrived, dad walked out with the help of an attendant. He wore a PPE kit. It all seemed so unreal and unbelievable; the things I had been hearing all over Delhi and in all the chat groups, all of it was happening in my life, and it looked a lot worse and more difficult. No matter how hard I tried to hold back my tears, they flowed non-stop. All I wanted was for him to be safe and fine, nothing more. As he sat in the ambulance and the door was shut, we set on a journey from home to the hospital that seemed way too long and hard. All you could hear was loud siren as we followed the ambulance all the way to the hospital. When we reached the hospital, the scene over there was even worse. There was a long queue of ambulances waiting to enter inside; one could only hear families crying, shouting, patients collapsing and see only unknown faces behind those PPE kits. Seeing all that, my heart sank and I felt I wasn't ready to leave dad all alone there in an unknown territory. I called my friend again and begged and cried for a better hospital of dad's choice, but my request could not be fulfilled. It just wasn't my day.

While dad anxiously waited in the recovery room for the formalities to be completed, I kept wondering where we were headed. All I wanted was to take him back home, but I didn't know what that decision would have led to. Keeping in mind his deteriorating health and his medical history, I just didn't have the courage to make such an uncertain call and take him back. During that entire waiting period, dad kept peeping from the recovery room and asking how long it would take. He was so restless and impatient by then that I remember after a point I had to hide behind a tree and watch him as I had no answer to his constant queries and didn't want him to get upset and tensed. When the formalities were over, they came out to take dad to his room. By then, he was seated on a wheelchair with an oxygen cylinder; I had never seen him like that. I spoke non-stop to dad; with the mask on, he definitely didn't see my uncontrollable tears flowing. I assured him that I would be back there soon to take him home, and he needed to stay strong and fight back. I reminded him he was my hero, and he just nodded his head before vanishing in front of my eyes inside the hospital. My last words to him were, "I am badly waiting to hug you tight and will do that in five days from now," as the hospital attendant had told us that dad would be home in five days. As he went inside, I kept talking and calling for him and saw him go for the LAST time with teary eyes far away from my sight.

'I haven't been able to fully catch my breath since the moment I watched you take your Last'

7

The Ordeal Began

When I look back at that day when I dropped dad at the hospital, I feel there was so much more I could have done or said. That day was the last time I ever saw him so close. Why did I hold myself back from hugging him and saying what I wanted to say to him?

Why didn't I see what was coming up next? Why didn't I realise the ordeal had just began and the road ahead was tougher and painful? Surprisingly, when I came back home after dropping dad, there was a sense of relief in me for the first time. I was hoping that dad would get better, now that he was in safe hands. He wasn't alone anymore as there were experienced people to look after him, and I told myself that was all I could have managed to do for him. I remember my cousin messaging me on my way back from the hospital, the message read, "Three cheers, Divya. You have done it! Now, the road ahead will be smooth and all will be ok very soon." Little did I know it wasn't going to be that easy at all.

It was the first day after April 24 that I actually slept at night. I felt dad would now be better soon because when I had spoken to dad a few hours after admitting him he had sounded better already. He told me the hospital looked very clean and nice from the inside, unlike what he had expected and was a bit impressed. It gave me so much relief. The next morning on 8 May, I called up dad to check on him, and to my surprise, he said he had slept peacefully after a very long time. He was finally a bit relieved as now he thought he had doctors to take care of him, but we didn't know that this happiness was short-lived.

Mom and my brother were discharged the very next day of dad's hospitalisation. Dad had waited for them to return for long so he could meet them, but fate had other plans. Now it was their turn to wait for dad to return home soon, a wait that never ended. Even today when I think about the extreme sense of loss that as a family we had felt — dad could not even meet his own wife and son in the last 15 days of his life just because they are were all fighting Covid — it feels just so miserable and unfair, something none of us had ever even imagined.

As we prayed hard for dad to settle in hospital and be well attended, things began to progress in the reverse direction. Dad's symptoms started to deteriorate, and owing to the rising pressure of COVID cases in the hospital, the level of assistance provided by the ground staff of the hospital began to degenerate. For someone who was always so used to the best of facilities and suite category room had to now wait for even a hot cup tea or his basic medication. Overburdened and exhausted staff was something that dad had not expected to deal with, but it was the reality of the sad state of Delhi at that time amidst the pandemic, and at home the helplessness that I felt was so tough to explain.

Dad had to wait for medication, food and even basic necessities as they were delayed or denied. For someone like dad, in that age and with his health condition, this was something very difficult to accept. No matter how hard we tried to pacify him and make him understand that all one could do to survive in a situation like that was adjust, it was very tough for dad to cope up all alone in a place completely new and unknown to him. Not a single familiar face or voice to calm him; by now, he was badly lost and scared. To make things even worse, dad got loose motions and had to make frequent visits to the bathroom, but the staff didn't help him with medication and oxygen support in the bathroom. No matter how much we begged and cried to him to use diapers, he refused to listen and continued to take off his oxygen support again and again to use the restroom as a result of which his oxygen level kept dropping. We ran from pillar to post, talked to the highest authorities inside the hospital and outside as well for help, but to no avail, and my poor dad suffered for it, both physically and emotionally. Finally, after a few hours, he actually received the required assistance even though things were manually controlled, but I know my dad had begun to lose faith and somewhere the battle to survive, too.

I do understand our sources were getting exhausted, hospital staff was tired and overburdened, but nothing at all could justify the trouble an old, weak man had to go through that day and in the days ahead. Not only did I lose my faith in the medical fraternity that day, but as a daughter it made me feel that had the medical authorities dealt with a little more compassion and humanity not only my dad but several others like him would have survived this pandemic and returned home. I do understand that the health infrastructure in the country was falling apart, but just a smile, a glass of water or a pat on the back would have meant so much to these patients like my dad; they would not have felt alone, unattended and most importantly, unloved.

Over the next two days, the situation went from bad to worse, and so did dad from five litre oxygen to 20 litre oxygen support. I made repeated calls to dad's floor to get just one piece of information, only to keep hearing one bad news after the other. Meanwhile, medically also things began to go out of control. Due to dad's weak liver, steroid administration had to be monitored and due to his need for high oxygen support, basic CT scan was also delayed, and things just went out of control one by one. When I called up dad, he was not even able to speak, badly breathless and tensed. The emotions in his voice were so clear every time. Finally, I decided not call him more as I didn't want to trouble him and feared he might remove the mask to talk to me, which I didn't want at all. Every hour, I would send him a voice note and the blue tick meant he had seen it, which was assurance enough to cope through the day.

The days and nights turned sleepless and tough to get through. Mom was very weak; she too was all alone and needed attention, and endless calls from friends and family for updates on dad kept pouring in, making it difficult to keep our sanity intact. Sometimes, it just felt like it was the worst nightmare and I wanted to immediately wake up from sleep and go back to the life I had until 23rd April. Nothing at all felt fine or right. On the third day, we received a call from the hospital informing us that dad was being shifted to the ICU. Unlike others, we weren't tensed at this development.

In fact, it brought us a sense of relief knowing that, at least now, dad would have 24-hour assistance, something that he needed badly. It was like running on a road with no directions and speed breaks and clueless about the destination. All we could do was just run to save our lives! Dad was in a lot of pain and was suffering. He was so troubled when he was getting pricked several times by the nurses as they would not find any veins because he had become so weak and drained. I still feel so anguished when I am reminded of that day when I called him to check on him and he shouted in agony that the nurses had been pricking him for a long time to get a blood sample but were unable to find the right vein. That cry of pain still haunts me.

Sometimes, I stop to think how does one make the right decision. After dad's passing away, I must have asked this to myself so many times. I went on the worst guilt trip wondering if I did the right thing to admit him. Would keeping him at home have been a better alternative? Initially, there was so much anger and frustration towards the system, but today, I think what else I could have done if not this. Being home, alone and without oxygen support and medical facilities, would that have been a more peaceful exit for dad from this world or the one he eventually had, bruised and pricked all over again and again for various tests and procedures done to maybe save him? WHAT would have been a better choice, I still ask myself a 100 times a day! A hard choice that so many like me made in those tough times all alone, taking over a burden of guilt for a lifetime.

Dad was always very scared of hospitals, blood tests or anything medically related. I remember, once mom had told me when I was young and had a bad attack of jaundice, I was so weak that I almost fainted. Before mom could react, seeing me in that condition, dad too fainted right there. Mom said she didn't even know whom to attend first, me or dad. He was very soft-hearted; he never accompanied anyone of us for any doctor visits and ran away if anyone ever had to get a blood test done. It just made me wonder every time there was a red code alert at the hospital how much my dad must have been traumatised. Meanwhile, inside the hospital, I managed to find a junior doctor and requested him to check on dad as we were unable to get any first-hand information, thanks to the language barrier that most of the hospital staff faced. Although we were getting regular updates from the hospital's chairman's office, due my dear friend, and also from the main doctor looking after him, somehow it wasn't enough to convince us. As that junior doctor went to check on dad, he let me speak to him. Even though dad was unwell, tired and scared, he still acted strong and said he would keep fighting. It was probably one of the LAST direct interactions I had with dad.

On the fourth day, he was moved to an NIV mask (mini ventilator) from the Bipap machine. His condition was deteriorating by the hour. I remember it was 10 May, and I waited all day to get any sign from dad. I didn't want to call and trouble him at all. Despite submitting every possible report and details about dad, the hospital staff still remained confused about his medical condition. This made the right treatment even more difficult to reach dad in time. It was a constant ordeal to explain every now and then what his body could take and what should be completely avoided in his case. Endless calls to contacts and connections, nothing was helping. It appeared by now that the hospital staff was overburdened and were literally following a set protocol for every patient suffering from COVID, and it didn't really matter to them how serious it could get for someone in particular with a serious underlying issue. No matter how hard I tried to tell myself that after all they were human too and were trying to do what they could to the best of their ability, the fact that doesn't change at all is that for the hospital, dad was just bed number four, nothing at all beyond that. To say they were emotionless would be harsh, but not completely wrong either. After all, what they were doing was only their duty, following their oath to the best of their ability. That old, weak patient didn't mean anything more to them, but for us, he was the centre of our universe our world… so, so precious!

Suddenly, in the midst of so much tension and chaos, I received a WhatsApp message from dad. It was around 5 pm in the evening, and he had replied to my voice notes from the morning. I can't say it made me happy, but it definitely lifted my spirits hearing from him. His every message gave me so much hope and filled me with enough positivity to carry on, no matter how terrible the situation was. Dad had replied back to my WhatsApp message with a thumbs up, and I immediately started messaging him back. I told him how much mom was missing him, to which he replied he knew that and he was missing her too. Then I told him he was my hero and I was waiting to hug him tight soon, to which dad replied with a red heart. I didn't realise at that time, but that heart was his LAST message to me. I never heard from him after that day, and the wait to receive that one more message will now be endless, for a lifetime. It was my dad's last and most special message. A heart, which actually was beating; he left me, he left all of us, but that beating heart will always be with me, reminding me of the boundless love and care he gave me as my darling father, my hero!

It was another restless night. All I could do was just pray for his speedy recovery. Non-stop chants and *mantra jaap* was all I could think and rely on. That day, I received a message to join a group of more than a 100 unknown people across the world and participate in *mahatraunjya jaap* to help all those people recover who were fighting COVID at that time.

oṃ tryámbakaṃ yajāmahe sugandhíṃ puṣṭi-vardhánam
urvārukam íva bandhánān mṛtyor mukṣīya mā 'mṛtāt

"We sacrifice to Tryambaka the fragrant, increaser of prosperity. Like a cucumber from its stem, might I be freed from death, not from deathlessness."

My heart suddenly felt it was God's way to show me a path that would take my dad on the road to recovery. So, I immediately signed up. And soon, I received another message that said that the *jaap* either helped you recover or helped the soul leave the body in peace without any pain and one should expect either of the two and remember that whatever happened would be the best option for the patient as per God's will.

For a moment, I was a bit taken aback as if I really wanted to do such a strong chant and what if the second option came true. But, the daughter in me took over and said, "Of course not. The first option of dad recovering will be true and my faith in God won't be ever be challenged, no matter what."

Next morning on 11 May, I woke up sharp at 6 am to participate in the chanting. As I chanted non-stop on Zoom with so many unknown people until 7 am, my tears flowed in fear, anxiety and love for dad. All I wanted was to just hear that dad was on a road to recovery. Post that, began the hustle to get new updates from doctors and attendants about dad's present condition, and so did the confusion regarding what medication was to be given to him and what to be avoided per his liver conditions. I saw dad online until 10.09 am and sent a few voice notes, which he didn't hear or replied to. In the afternoon, I received a call from the hospital that the doctor wanted to meet one of the family members, and we were expected to sign consent papers for plasma to be administered to dad as well as arrange the lifesaving drug tocilizumab for dad at the earliest. This scared us a lot as it was a very strong drug and was in high demand, and hence, not easily available.

Then began a series of endless phone calls to friends and family to arrange the injection as soon as possible. And soon, we got an update from one of dad's friends that it was arranged and that too not from the black market but from the company that was making and supplying the drug in India. The drug was arranged at no cost as they valued their relationship with dad. Suddenly, a part of me had so much gratitude for God, and I began to think that nothing could go wrong as God was right there to help us and protect dad. As my brother and I got ready to rush to the hospital, Manish suggested that we should definitely go and meet dad in the ICU. My heart skipped a beat at those words. Why did he say that? Why was it needed? After all, entering the ICU was not only impossible but a great risk as it was highly infectious. But he said we must make the effort or we would regret it all our life. So, I packed all the necessary things such as the shield, PPE kits, masks and gloves for the same and went prepared to the hospital in the hopes of meeting dad.

When we reached the hospital, we were made to meet the head pulmonologist at the hospital who was treating dad. As he sat us down and spoke about dad in detail, somehow I felt all was under control and things would look up in the positive direction soon. He told us dad's medical condition was under control and he was responding well to the medication and treatment. According to him, although there were complications, he still felt dad had an amazing fighting spirit and would definitely bounce. He also told us how famous our dad was and that he was receiving so many messages from so many influential people all over Delhi to get regular updates about everyone's favourite Suresh bhai and how he was doing in the hospital. He told us quite light-heartedly that we should tell everyone not to bother the doctor and let him do his job.

The doctor also said that every time he visited, dad would acknowledge him with a smile and shining eyes full of hope as he could not speak because he was on very high oxygen support and could not remove the mask even for a second. All this and more was shared in that 25-30 minute meeting. Lastly, he told us that if all went well, things should be in control in the following two to three days and dad should start recovering. All these words suddenly gave me so much hope and I told myself that now dad will surely be home soon. And why would he not? After all, dad was double vaccinated too! Yes, he had got both shots of vaccine well in time and every one told us that, eventually, the jabs would help him recover and nothing fatal would happen.

As we walked out with a new sense of hope and positivity, Manish reminded us to go to the ICU, and I told him about the conversation with the doctor and how hopeful he was of dad's speedy recovery and that a visit was not needed. Dad should be fine in the next two to three days. As we drove back home, leaving dad back in the hospital, I didn't know it was the last time I was so close to dad and that he might be waiting to see us for one last time. As soon as I sat in the car, my evil-eye bracelet broke. I still took it as a positive sign and hoped something evil had passed by and all would be fine soon. Throughout our way back home Manish remained angry with me for not making that effort to meet dad, but I just could not explain to him the mixed emotions I had. On the one hand, I was dying to see him and on the other hand, I didn't want to do anything that could have triggered any bigger issue; seeing us could have got dad excited or restless, anything could have happened. The reactions and actions at this stage just could not have been predicted, and I was definitely not ready to take any risk at all. Strangely, I came back home a bit calmer, but the only thing that kept troubling me was that I had not seen dad online post 10.09 am that day. As I got busy making calls to arrange a plasma donor for dad the next day, my heart kept waiting for one update on WhatsApp, and my anxiety remained high.

By evening, I got an update from the management that plasma had been given to him, but that dad had also developed pneumonia. Unable to understand the medical terminology, I realised much later what it meant. I continued the rest of the day with non-stop chanting and prayers for dad, just hoping and wishing for a miracle. As night came closer, my restlessness grew as I was waiting to hear from dad badly. As

Manish, Manya and I sat to pray, my tears just couldn't stop and neither could my growing fear. As I was praying, I started to visualise a beautiful *satsang* when dad would return home! Not only did I think of the colours of the *Chola* (dress) I would make my beloved *Guruji* wear, but I also imagined the floral combinations too. As my mind got a bit distracted with these beautiful thoughts, it felt a little better and the idea of planning a *satsang* brought me so much hope and comfort.

That night, I could not sleep. I felt lost and jittery, and above all, alone. Mom wasn't able to talk to me at all as she was so week, unwell and tensed because of dad, and there was no update from dad. That night Manish suggested that I slept alone as I had been to the hospital and was getting exposed to the infection again and again; it wasn't safe for our daughter. So, we all slept in different rooms that night. It was terrible. I turned left and right and in possibly all directions. My eyes just refused to blink even for a moment, and I literally felt like an insomniac, and just then, the phone rang.

I still clearly remember it was 5:23 am on the clock, and I picked the phone on the first ring. I even recognised it was from the hospital, even though I hadn't saved the number yet; I had started to recognise the area code. As I picked up the phone, my heartbeat increased uncontrollably, and someone spoke on the other side. As God had planned it, the name of the doctor on the other side of the phone was also Divya! As she spoke, I got more and more impatient. The first thing she asked was that if I was Mr. Suresh Gupta's attendant. I said yes, and then, she asked my relationship with him and I said I was his daughter. She asked if someone else was in the room with me. I'll have to admit I had started to lose my edge and had started to feel very uneasy. In fact, just then my gut feeling said that now she would say that due to some complications my dad was on the ventilator. I really don't know why I suddenly felt like that, but somehow, I had been hearing the same all over from everyone who was unwell in the known circle. I felt she would say the same, and while my mind thought of all this horrible stuff, she asked again if there was someone else in the room. I replied that I was alone. I asked her to tell me what the matter was as I wasn't able to handle the stress and suspense anymore. And then Dr. Divya said my dad had suffered a cardiac arrest a little while ago. I was confused, and I asked her how it was even possible, for my dad wasn't even a heart patient. As I failed to understand the details, she didn't want to explain it either. She said that as a result of the attack and after continuously providing CPR for twelve to fifteen minutes, they had eventually given up as there was NO response from dad.

There was a strange silence as she said she was SORRY and that my dad, my hero, my everything was NO MORE. He was gone! My ears had just heard the most unimaginable and cruellest words ever. My dad was GONE leaving me behind. Gone forever, never to return again. It was all over.

It just felt very strange. It was something I had never imagined to hear. It sounded so unbelievable. The way things were shaping up, the way dad's health was deteriorating day by day and the way things were in Delhi at that time, as an outsider anyone could see it coming, but a daughter's mind and heart was just not ready to accept it. How could someone with whom I had exchanged a message just a day ago, whom I had myself gone to drop at the hospital, someone with whom I had spent the past two weeks so closely was gone so suddenly?

My heart just asked me one question at that moment for the first time, "WHY ME, GOD?" After years of worship, dedication, connection and true faith in the divine power, how could god choose me to go through this tragedy and that too in this way? Suffering and pain are things that heal our past life's karma's, but I had never imagined that the end would be so heartbreaking.

My heart just refused to accept that my dad was no more, that I wouldn't get to see him ever again and the hug for which I waited so much in those last few days, that hug I would never get. Just as the realisation of these things hit me hard, I screamed and ran to Manish's room. He immediately woke up and took the phone from me and spoke to the doctor further. He requested them to try again, try more, but I guess they had already given up on him before they even called us.

As I howled looking at the sky from the room window, I felt my dad going away from me forever. I would never be able to see him and touch him again. The feeling killed me a thousand times that day, and what made it even worse was that excruciating pain I experienced for the first time of having become a fatherless daughter. An immediate emptiness made me numb. As we all cried together, Manya, Manish and me, holding each other for support, just then, the worst feeling in the world struck me. I had never even imagined that I would be the one to inform my family about dad's departure. As a daughter, I always thought as I stayed in a different house, I would get a call one day informing that dad was not well or something similar, but as I was the only attendant for him at the hospital, this difficult task was also given to me by God to break it to my family and experience the most horrifying pain. Even as I write about that fateful morning, my throat gets badly choked with emotions as that day would never vanish from my mind as my worst day ever. After that for days, weeks and months, I remember I would wake up every morning at the same time when that phone had rang from the hospital and had changed my life forever.

That one phone call changed everything forever; nothing has felt the same after that. So much grief surrounded our lives that it is still difficult to fathom the intensity of the pain at times. I was not the only one I know, and I reminded myself so many times after that fateful day, but sometimes, you just lose the power to even think and accept things the way they are. Loss of a father slowly becomes a wound that can never be healed, and no amount of time has the power to fill that void ever. Suddenly, seeing normal happy people makes you angry; the triggers are everywhere. There is a constant struggle to see your loved one, to go back to their old pictures and messages; zoom into each picture every time and hope to see them alive once again; and then, go over and over things wondering if any of it is even real and hoping there is no more bad news coming up soon. There is a constant insecurity that surrounds your life and it is just so painful.

The timeline of grief is weird; our lives stop unnoticeably, while everyone's else's continues; then, you wake up realising how long it has been, how many days and months have gone by and you wonder how you even made it there!

8

Our Last Goodbye Was Never Said!

As I sit down to write today, I still can't believe it has been so long since I lost dad. It is 12 November 2021, and who says time flies. It feels like it had all happened yesterday so quickly that I still at times can't believe how fast COVID had taken over our lives, leaving behind a scar for a lifetime.

Like losing dad wasn't painful enough, what made it even worse was not getting any closure for our feelings. Not being able to mourn over the death of your loved one the way a family would have wanted, made this farewell even more unbearable. I still remember on 11 May as we were unable to get any clarity on dad's condition and things were getting more and more critical, I had sat down to pray to *Guruji*. On the one hand, as a daughter I just prayed for his speedy recovery and on the other hand, a part of me again and again begged *Guruji* that no matter what happened dad should not go with COVID.

A person who had lived his life with so much dignity and had spread so much love and positivity, who had always stood by people in their good and bad times and supported everyone in need, didn't deserve to go like that at all. I told *Guruji* that even if it was his time to go, for one last time he should be granted one more year of life for all the deeds he had done. No matter what, he should not go with COVID as it was one death that would not only break us as a family but my dad's soul would also be hurt for departing in so much silence all alone, without any loved one around during his last moments.

Dad liked living larger than life. He always loved family and friends around him, and to even begin to imagine a COVID death for him was one of the biggest shocks for us. What I had heard and watched on TV and phone during the second wave of pandemic now looked closer to home. All I had wanted, if nothing else, was that dad should at least depart in style surrounded by so much love that his journey ahead would be peaceful and less painful. I prayed to God to grant me the blessing of cutting my fortieth birthday cake in January 2022 with my dad. That would have been the biggest gift of my life, had it come true. But life and destiny are not in our hands. As much as my heart prayed and begged for God's mercy and blessings, the most inevitable pain was around the corner and none of my wishes were granted at the end or as I thought so at that moment of extreme sadness.

After trying to deal with the unfathomable emotions that came with the loss, the next thought that came to mind was how we would say our last goodbye to him in such a bad situation that COVID had created. Things were beyond anyone's control, and nothing looked easy and doable at that moment. As we struggled hard to get our thoughts together and prepare to arrange for this most difficult task of my life, so much began to break inside me. No amount of tears were enough to wash away the pain that the one phone call from the hospital had brought with it. And then, started the ordeal of running around to arrange things to ensure a peaceful departure for dad in those challenging times when to arrange an ambulance, crematorium or even performing simple rituals felt like an unthinkable task.

Every now and then, my heart would stop to think if it was actually happening to me. The phone rang non-stop like it had never before. Concerned friends and family from across the globe were trying to reaching out to us with their words of consolation and grief, but we had nothing to say, nothing left to update! Moreover, most were shocked at the news because all this while dad had hidden his condition from most of his well-wishers as he only wanted to focus on the recovery of the rest of the family that was hospitalised. He didn't want people to direct their concern towards him as he was all alone at home at that time. Every time I asked him why he was hiding, he would laugh and say that as it was the phone had been constantly ringing, if his loved ones got to know about his health, they would go crazy and would want to check on him and it would be him who would go mad attending all the panic calls. So now, I too was left to deal with the never-ending questions and anger from loved ones who felt cheated that dad had hid it from all of them all this while. I feel even worse that because he hid it from so many, he missed out on so many prayers that were truly meant for him and he simply passed them on for the rest of the family and for their safety.

The phone kept ringing, messages kept pouring in and social media and school and college networks had actively spread the news all over within a few hours. But, our hearts were silent as there was just nothing left to say. All this while, I had tried my best to give updates to everyone who called me about my family as much as I could and as much as dad had allowed me to do, but that day I had no words. I was speechless. I almost froze with the thought of not being able to see my dear dad ever again. It felt as if a happy world had just crashed down, a castle had broken and lost its king so suddenly and definitely untimely.

That day, the pain I experienced was unexplainable; I had never felt anything like it before. And then, began a guilt trip that took me on a road of never-ending questions that I repeatedly asked myself. As I was the only one with dad during those last days, I asked myself so many times if the decisions I took were correct. Did I do anything wrong? What went wrong? Why after so much effort I could not save the most precious person of my life? I felt so cheated as if I had failed the most important exam of my life, an exam I could never be allowed take again. I hated myself for taking the most important decision of his life, something that I had never done before, and was unable to perform to the best of my capacity. How was he when he was in the ICU? Was he in a lot of pain? The most important question that almost broke me on the inside was how he had been in his last few moments when he was all alone with not even one family member close to him. How unbearable this feeling must have been for dad? Was he upset with me for I had promised to get him back home safe, back to his son and wife? This and so many more questions shattered my existence as much as the news of dad's death did. What would have you done if you were in my shoes? Did you see another way out of this crazy situation that I had got into since 24 April. Can you tell me if there was a better plan to deal with all this and maybe come out victorious?

As I blamed myself more and more, there was just no end to my thoughts that flowed completely unstoppable. But what had happened had happened and even if I refused to accept it, it was impossible to reverse the loss. Just then, the daughter in me felt there was still the slightest chance of this cruel news being wrong. What if the hospital had made a mistake? What if it wasn't dad in bed number four? So, I decided to go and see dad for one last time in the hopes of finding that it wasn't really him. The crazy, inconsolable daughter inside me had this thought. Even today, at times when I sleep, I get shivers thinking how tough that situation was and how unmanageable the circumstances were, making a COVID-hit family so helpless and alone, with many still waiting for closure that they never got.

I told Manish that I would be accompanying him to the crematorium. He didn't say anything as he understood very well how tough this decision was for me in the first place, but as soon as my mom got to know about my plan, despite her condition, she called me and ordered me not to go. In our family and the Hindu community, the daughters and the ladies of the family don't visit the place of cremation as per the custom, so she didn't want me to go either. She said if I went, she would not talk to me all her life. I told her that I was okay with that, but I would not agree to stay back at any cost. It was my one last chance to see dad and I wasn't ready to let it go at any cost! I just hung up the phone, refusing to obey my mom for the first time ever. What followed was the preparation to meet dad for one last time in the most strange circumstances.

As Manish and I got dressed in full PPE kits and left home, the feeling of that emptiness was unexplainable. I left behind my daughter crying to see her dear *nanu* for the last time. As a family, it was so difficult to deal with things that would not give you any closure for years to come. How could you send off someone like that, without even meeting or seeing, without him even coming back to his house for one last time, without even his complete family by his side on his farewell, a family that dad had always held so close to his heart? There had been so much suffering in last few days, so was this the finale?

That drive to the Lodhi crematorium felt never ending. I remembered the siren of the ambulance that I had followed just five days before; till then I had so much hope and positivity and today it was all over! As we reached Lodhi, my eyes could not help but see the biggest irony of life: on the left side of the road was dad's favourite place to hang out, the Lodhi hotel, and on the right side of the road was the crematorium where he was to be brought for his cremation, where I would lose him forever. As the ambulance approached the gate of the crematorium, my heart started pumping loudly. It felt as if dad had come and the emotions were uncontrollable. As the ambulance stopped inside the gate and I gathered the courage to walk towards it, the heaviness inside me became unbearable. And there he was! My dad, my hero, wrapped in a white hospital bag, lying so quietly. As I saw him from the window, I screamed and shouted for his attention. I had seen him after five days of endless wait and this visual was something I could never have imagined in my entire life.

He lay inside all calm and I kept banging on the window calling out his name. I told him his Cheenu was here and why was he sleeping like that; why on earth was he so quiet for the first time ever. I kept apologising for being unable to save him after so much effort and failing to fulfil my promise of getting him back. I spoke and spoke but for the first time dad didn't reply! All my life, I had heard dad speaking, but it was so different and difficult this time. I could not bear the feeling that dad wasn't replying at all. The hospital bag said his name loud and clear. As I stood helpless outside the van, my heart underwent so much turmoil that is was tough to control the flow of emotions. I could not believe that it was happening to us and most importantly to dad. It was such a lonely sight; just his two children, their life partners and a few office staff were able to attend his last journey, unlike what it actually would have been if it wasn't for the pandemic.

Given the love that dad had spread all his life and the relationships he had built, his last rites would have attracted a crowd of hundreds if the situation were normal. The traffic of cars and the noise of well-wishers would have been uncontrollable, unlike what it actually looked like that day. Dad always taught us to stand by people in difficult times even if we couldn't be a part of their happiness. He felt those who showed up in the hour of need were any day more special than who only came to share your joy and success. As long as dad lived, he never missed any opportunity to attend funerals of his loved ones. It didn't matter to him whether it was freezing cold or scorching heat, whether he was unwell or busy, dad would always take out time for such commitments. He would always be the first one to reach and offer a shoulder to cry on or even take up responsibilities so that the person in need could be helped. Dad had a very particular habit, every morning he would read the obituary section in the paper without fail, and so he would never miss the funerals of anyone he knew or was connected with.

It was unbelievable to see dad's funeral being held in such sad times when nobody could come and pay their last respects to a person who truly deserved it. Although friends and family had gathered outside the crematorium, they were forced to remain in their cars as the government rules didn't allow people to attend the funeral for safety concerns. The ambulance attendant saw our situation and agreed to show us dad's face for one last time. Suddenly, a ray of hope sparked inside me: what if it wasn't dad, what if this was just not true? As he began to open the packed bags, my heart began to sink. It was a situation that I might never be able to express in words. He opened the first layer, then the second and finally, the third, and there it was, I saw my dad's face. As we all howled and cried, he lay there so quietly and with so much calmness on his face, grown white bread and salt and pepper hair. Dad had finally LEFT us all and what I saw was the last glimpse of the face, that smile that always lighted up my life, my existence.

My last hope to be proved wrong and witness a miracle was shattered. My dashing and handsome dad, always well-dressed, now lay so lifeless in that ambulance packed in those hospital bags. I could never have imagined that life could be so unpredictable and so unfair. Someone who deserved to get the grandest of farewells, surrounded by so much love and warmth was leaving alone and quiet. As per the Hindu customs, whenever a loved one departs, the family offers shawls and flowers, but my dad left in those hospital bags. He didn't even get enough shoulders to carry his coffin to his final destination. The grief of seeing dad go like that will never end and will remain in my heart forever. No amount of words will ever be enough to console this throbbing pain I received that day seeing him leave like that.

Seeing dad's face so calm and peaceful did bring some consolation that a special soul like him had now travelled to another world to serve his higher purpose. He had gone to a place where he was needed more and loved more. He was always God's favourite. Even though he had faced numerous hardships and struggles in life, there was always a divine power that helped him succeed in whatever he did and achieve all what he eventually had. As I saw him, the volcano of emotions exploded and was almost uncontrollable. As the scorching heat slowly combined with extremely high emotions, the day became so much more difficult to survive, being packed inside those PPE kits. We were badly drenched in sweat and tears and felt so helpless like never before. For a moment, I felt I would just faint and won't even be able to walk back to my car. Post that, I just went and sat in a corner on the crematorium pavement as it felt all was over now and nothing was left to think and pray for. They took dad towards the main cremation area and whatever limited last rites could be performed were done by my brother and husband. I saw dad being surrendered to the holy fire; slowly, it surrounded his body and soon dad's physical form turned into ashes. As I write this, I am overwhelmed with emotions because for a daughter that was an unimaginable sight. Every time I think about that tragic day, something breaks inside me. Although it was entirely my decision to be a part of dad's last rites, it was the most difficult and painful experience for me and the visuals shall hound me for the rest of my life.

Grief is unexplainable unless you have experienced it yourself, you will never truly know the pain that consumes you when someone you love more than anything on earth dies.

Why is it so difficult to let your loved one go? I have asked this question to myself numerous times since that day. We all know we are not immortal, and, eventually, we will all go. That's the reality of life, yet when we actually face death, we are never prepared for it. As a child I had heard many times that God calls them soon whom he loves the most, was my dad God's most loved child? I quietly watched dad's final departure from this world with a smile on his face and shine in his eyes, and I left the crematorium with a very heavy heart, leaving behind my dad whom I could not even meet, speak, touch, hug and say my last goodbye.

'You lose a part of yourself, when you lose someone you love'

As I returned home, it felt like I had missed him forever now. But in reality, this was just the beginning of a lifetime of missing him. The emptiness and the unnatural pain that I felt inside me that day was not easy to express in words. It was tough to absorb that at 5:23 am I had got the call from the hospital about dad and by 11:30 all his last rites were performed and by 12:30 we were even back home. Why was God in so much hurry to take dad away from us? Why didn't we as a family get enough time to mourn our biggest loss and bid him a final adieu the way one could have imagined in normal circumstances?

The most painful goodbyes are the ones that are never said and never explained.

9

Farewell

No words for farewell were spoken; there was no time to say goodbye. You were gone before we knew it and only God knows why.

As if dealing with the anguish of losing dad wasn't enough, I even had to deal with the pain of losing him to a disease that changed our lives forever. Had my family not been hit by the pandemic so badly, I am sure dad would have lived longer. Together, there was so much more we could have done: spent more fun lunches at Lodhi, celebrated more birthdays and festivals together or just heard him a little more over calls and messages.

His passing away left me bitter and angry, and I often asked myself, "WHY US?" What did we do so wrong to go through all this? Karma, maybe? How am I ever supposed to feel confident, safe and secure when the person who validated me the most was no longer around? .It's like losing someone who made me feel safe, loved, who had my back, who gave advices, who taught so much. Losing this most precious relationship is definitely bound to have a massive effect on one's ability to now know who you are, how to trust yourself and others now.

As we left from the Lodhi crematorium, I didn't know there was more suffering to come. As if this pain wasn't enough to deal with, I began thinking of my mom.

All this while I was so caught up with looking after dad that I had just forgotten about her, but now she was all I had. My precious mom was my only parent now. As mom was still COVID-positive, even after getting discharged from the hospital, I was advised not to go close to her — another difficult advice to take. How could you not go and meet your own mother when you have just lost your father? It was something I needed, and my heart went out to her as my poor mom didn't even get to see her husband of 42 years one last time. Unlike us, mom had lived with him all these years, through all good and bad times, happy and sad moments, served all his needs, cooked all his meals and remained his biggest strength. Her presence in dad's life was so important that the moment she left for the hospital, dad became so lonely and he actually could not survive without her.

As mom was extremely unwell and weak after her return from the hospital, she was in no condition to go to the funeral. It was her biggest loss; she had lost her life partner and that too to COVID. They were not even together in the last 12 days before dad passed away. My mom saw dad last on 27 April when she left for the hospital, and by the time she returned home, dad was hospitalised. She waited anxiously for him to return, but her wait never ended and dad never came back home. Dad had come out in the balcony to see her off and he was the one who had forced me to hospitalise her as he could not see her suffer alone isolated in the room. Mom cried inconsolably wondering why did she even leave dad in the first place and went away from him for the first time in so many years of being married.

Mom was dad's lucky charm. We always heard and saw it with regards to business, but that day I realised she was also his lucky charm when it came to his life. How I wish I knew it before and they would not have been separated like this from each other in such sad circumstances. They were a sweet and simple couple; they had their shares of agreements and disagreements and led a simple life always dedicated to their kids and their families. My mom was always a homemaker and she saw no life beyond it without dad. From morning tea to playing cards during the lockdown, from fighting over senseless issues to spending time together, whatever they did, they always did it together. And now, even to begin to imagine mom without dad was so painful. Theirs was not a romantic bond, but there was something that held them together so strongly for all these years against all odds.

As all these thoughts crossed my mind on my way back from the crematorium, Manish parked the car outside my mom's house. As I wasn't allowed to meet her, I called her out to the balcony to have a look at her. When she came out, we both cried so helplessly that day, unable to speak or meet. Why had god punished us this way? I told her to take care of herself and said that I could not get dad back with me. For the first time, we both fell short of words to express the emotions we were going through a that moment. After that, I came back home feeling so incomplete and defeated. It was one of the heaviest and most disturbing days of my life. For the rest of the day, I continued to stay lifeless and numb trying to swallow down what had just happened.

The next day, the family began to think about dad's prayer meeting and many thoughts began to cross my mind. My dad's prayer meeting on Zoom? I could never have imagined that. My dad always wished for a very grand prayer meeting! Yes, I know how strange this must sound but he always wanted a very well-organised prayer meeting. Once, he had even mentioned that whenever he would go, we should book the best venue in town like Taj Palace Hotel, get the most beautiful floral decorations, hire the best singer and, most importantly, cater the best food to all his friends and family when he was gone. And today, we didn't know how to do anything at all, with the pandemic still raging on.

It brought me so much grief that as a family we were unable to complete his last wish of departing in style. My dad always made sure that he attended each and every prayer meeting he could. For him, it was more important than any other social commitments. Unlike most of us, he would not reach in the last 10 minutes just to register his presence; he would become a part of everyone's sorrow as much as he could and stand by them to give a shoulder to cry on. I always felt what he did was so special. Often, dad and I would meet at common prayer meetings and I would see how involved and concerned he used to be for the family of the deceased.

He would always maintain that we could miss any happy occasions, any happy moment could be compensated with your love and gestures, and no wonder he never gave much importance to destination weddings or parties. But he would never miss an opportunity to be a part of any sad occasion. Like so many others who passed away during COVID, he didn't get the farewell he truly deserved. We could not bring him home from the hospital one last time, to the house he loved so much, where he stayed in his last few days before he left all of us. He could not come back to his wife, his kids and grandchildren for one last time, leaving without so many final goodbyes.

And why wouldn't I feel bad? After all, the extraordinary life he lived, the love that he gave and the values and principles he upheld, and the concern he showed for people in both good and bad times definitely had to be remembered through his prayer meeting. But instead of celebrating a pure soul like dad for one last time, we were left with no choice but to just stay silent with tears in our eyes and memories in our hearts for him.

Again, as destiny had planned, I was given the responsibility of planning dad's Zoom prayer meeting. Despite the emotional turmoil we were all going through, I tried my best to manage whatever I could. On the day of his prayer meeting, I had goosebumps; it felt so uncomfortable that words might fall short to explain it. And I got fever; my family thought that I had also began to show symptoms of COVID as I had been badly exposed in the last few days. Later, it turned out the fever was due to extreme anxiety and stress that I was going through while trying to wear so many hats together. To everyone's biggest surprise, even after being repeatedly exposed to high degree of infection, I didn't contract Covid during the second wave when even a handshake or sneeze was enough to catch the infection. And here I was fighting against all odds. Today, it feels this was also God's will that he kept me safe in such a hostile situation so that I could handle all the stress and tasks alone. My purpose of existing at that time was surely different as per God's will.

When the meeting began and I saw my dad's picture on the screen, there was yet another emotional outburst. What made it even more painful was that despite being his only daughter I wasn't allowed to attend it in person with the rest of the family as they all were still COVID-positive. The helplessness of attending it from my house and not being able to offer flowers to his picture in person broke me even more. Everyone who joined had tears and a sense of pain prevailed in the meeting room. As the singer Ankit Batra sang for dad, the smell of his favourite flower *rajnigandha* surrounded me even though I wasn't there in person. The terrible feeling of seeing your own mom and family on screen and not being able to be with them was painful. As I quietly watched his picture that was kept in front of me in my house, all I could do was apologise to dad for being unable to give him the send-off he had always wanted.

Throughout the meeting, people from across the globe, his friends, family and so many loved ones joined in a very large number, almost touching 500 and more on Zoom and through the YouTube link. So many also wrote about him in the chat box. Some shared their experiences with him, some spoke about how and when dad made a difference in their lives, whereas some just remembered him so fondly and expressed their sadness at such a big and untimely loss. Together, we all mourned the loss of a precious life to the pandemic. At the end of the meeting, the coordinator tried his best that I unmute and say something about dad, but it was just impossible for me. By then, I was so badly chocked with emotions that to say anything for my beloved dad seemed just out of question. All this while, I had waited for things to get back to normal, and here I was attending my father's prayer meeting. It felt like the battle was so badly lost. It felt like an end of an era. It pained me to imagine had things gone back to normal, had dad recovered like the rest of the family members, this day would have been so different. Dad would have been so happy to be back with his family and would have been so proud of his daughter for holding the fort so strongly all alone. And here I was instead, all defeated, exhausted, tired and lost. Surprisingly, after the meeting, so many well-wishers messaged us saying that they truly loved the homage that was paid to dad that evening and they were so touched and driven by emotions. In fact, for many days or even after months, I had people mentioning to me about this unusual tribute that had truly touched their hearts. Some even inquired about details when they too had a loss and wanted to make it as beautiful as this one for their loved one.

But it didn't stop there. For the real king of hearts, my dad, who touched so many lives, who added spark to so many gatherings, what followed was several more such farewells, prayers meetings for many days organised by MSOSA, his 1970 school batchmates, St. Stephen's College, the FMS community and other groups that dad was always very closely attached to. They too showed their love and fondness for him in their own way.

People got together to remember him, to talk about him and to tell others what made him so special. Each and every one had so much to share and so much to talk about dad. Some called him a livewire and expressed disbelief at the loss of their true friend; some said that he would now be networking up in the heaven and would still get everyone together. Some even said that he would never rest in peace and would continue to keep spreading his warmth, affection and his infectious energy wherever he would go. Friends from all walks and stages of life came together to celebrate him. They talked about how hardworking he was and how he had been the only link between so many batchmates for all these years. They all remembered their dear old, ever-so-charming Suresh so fondly, and just when I was struggling to collect more and more memories of dad from my phone gallery during one of his farewell meetings, they played a beautiful poem sung by dad himself that he sang during the online celebration of his golden jubilee last year. This poem in dads own voice was one of the most beautiful treasures I received that day!

A few old friends remembered his struggles when he was young and how he had worked hard to become a successful entrepreneur, whereas others spoke about how giving and large-hearted person he was, who never valued money over relationships. He was someone whom many remembered for his unlimited contributions and donations for good causes whenever he could. However, what most remembered him for was his smiling face, warm nature and tight hugs that he always showered his loved ones with. My most dapper and handsome dad was spoken about by so many that I felt so proud of him. On some occasions, I wondered if I really knew what my dad, Mr. Suresh Gupta, actually was as a human being. As his daughter, for the first time, I felt I knew so little about him and so much was still left to learn from him. For the first time, I felt my own dad was a book by himself that I had not actually got an opportunity to read all these years!

He didn't just enjoy organising reunions but he also used to push others to do so, and it was heart-breaking to know that when the batch finally got together, it was for his own prayer meeting. They all shared the same sad emotion that the batch was together not for a celebration but to remember the most loved one who had left so soon and in such an unbelievable way. Every tear from his loved ones' eyes expressed so much love for dad. What hit me even more was that so many things, instances and deeds came to light in these prayer meetings that we as a family were unaware of. Dad never made us realise what he actually was, what made him more special than others. Why do we always tend to take people around us for granted and forget to tell them how much we actually love them? We keep waiting for the right time to do so, until it's too late. We only realise their true worth once they are gone!

Not that I didn't know how important dad was in my life, how invaluable he was for me, but I never knew he was the same or even more for many others whose life he had invariably touched over the years with his gestures and warmth. It was unbelievable to see so many people from different stages of his life, different age groups and professional backgrounds come together to mourn the loss of a loved one who had always helped them and stood by them. Dad wore multiple hats, not only was he an amazing dad but also a lovable husband and rocking grandad. He was also the best friend, batchmate, colleague anyone could have asked for. He was the perfect client that his partners loved dealing with again and again. He would not bargain but leave behind tips and suggestions instead to grow their business better. He was a great business associate who would never think of spoiling someone else's order to make some more money or cheat in dealings. He was the best teacher, from whom many young and budding entrepreneurs had taken some of the best lessons of life and business to grow and reach to the heights they were at today. He was always a giver, a great person! No wonder he was respected by so many all over. And each and every person spoke so fondly of him in every prayer meeting for him that took place to not only remember him but to actually celebrate the life he had lived.

He was a gifted human being. He left behind not only so many beautiful memories and experiences that one can learn from and succeed in life, but also his values and beliefs. His never-say-die spirit is something to be followed by generations to come. He taught so much with his exemplary life; for him no work was big or small, and he believed that no one should shy away from hard work if they wanted to do well in life. There was no substitute for hard work and honesty in his books. Starting from a small factory in Wazirpur area to cracking the best business deals later, he was always ready to take risks and give his best. No loss at work or deception in business deals ever could break his determination to bounce back and do even better next time. And most importantly, in a world where relationships are short-lived and measured with the social status of a person, there lived a man, my dad, who in his extraordinary way nurtured so many beautiful bonds and continued to hold on to them as long as he lived.

Despite the numerous farewells that dad got, my heart still felt empty. A daughter's heart can never say goodbye to her most precious relationship, her dad. So, as everyone spoke and remembered him so emotionally and fondly, I wanted to do something different. As I say this, I am well aware that we were not alone in those testing times. Just like us, so many more had gone through the worst time of their lives and were equally shattered and left alone to weep. The thought that eventually dad might be forgotten as life moved on haunted me for days. Regardless of how hard I might try to hold on to his valuable memories, save his messages, try and preserve his smell in his last worn clothes, everything will somehow fade. The constant fear of losing anything that reminded me of him refused to leave my mind. The more I thought, the more it shattered me. I will only have few pictures as my only biggest treasure. With every bit of happiness or joy in my life in future, I'll get a lump in my throat and deep sadness in my heart knowing that I can never share that news with him ever again. I know the pain and insecurities the immediate family feels are unbearable and the loss is unrepairable and that's why I decided my hero deserved a farewell that was as unique and as special as him.

I always felt dad had the right spark to be a politician or a page 3 personality. The fact that he was so famous proves my point. How he managed to know so many people and that too from so many different walks of life is a marvel. Someone like him had to be celebrated and remembered for years to come, and that's how the idea of this book was born! Yes, the right farewell for my super popular dad by his daughter as her last attempt to make him proud. With this book I wanted him to live on in our hearts and memories. When memory would begin to fade away with age and good deeds would be forgotten by many, my memoir would keep him alive. A gift for generations to come so that his legacy, values and beliefs could continue. Every time I would miss the warmth of his love and the shelter of his guidance, this book would bring him close to me and comfort me. This collection of his teachings, experiences and his memories would never ever fade away with the passing days, months and years. This was my way of paying tribute to him as his proud daughter. Although his infectious energy, winning personality, happy smile and warm hugs shall remain irreplaceable for years to come, through this book, he would definitely live on forever and ever. The story of his journey, achievements, his relationships and his sparkling diamond-like aura through my eyes and in my words was my ideal farewell to my rock star dad, who lived the life of a king with an irreplaceable crown!

I believe that keeping an account of people's lives is really about making sure they are remembered through their stories even when they are no more.

न जायते म्रियते वा कदाचि नायं भूत्वा भविता वा न भूय: ।
अजो नित्य: शाश्वतोऽयं पुराणो न हन्यते हन्यमाने शरीरे ॥

A loving husband and beloved father,
***Mr. Suresh Gupta** has left us for heavenly abode*

Mr. Suresh Gupta
(12.03.1953 - 12.05.2021)

He lived life so cheerfully, always lent a selfless helping hand, was ever patient and never looked back with regret. His zeal for life was contagious. He extended a helping hand to whoever came to him, never leaving empty handed. As many Moderniites and Stephanians would attest, his radiant ebullient life deserves to be beautifully remembered as one lived with contentment, patience and inner strength.

Those we love don't go away, they walk beside us. Everyday, unseen, unheard, but always near. Still loved, still missed and very dear. If tears could build a staircase and memories a lane, I'd walk right upto Heaven and bring You home again.

PLEASE CLICK THE YOUTUBE & ZOOM LINK

zoom
Zoom Meeting ID: 821 1815 7734, Passcode: 1234
Saturday, May 15, 2021 Time: 05:00 PM
YouTube

With profound grief

Anju Gupta
Wife

Dipesh and Shagun Gupta
Son and Daughter-in-law

Divya and Manish Kotawala
Daughter and Son-in-law

Veer, Vedaanti, Manya
Grandchildren

Dad's prayer meeting on zoom on 15th may 2021

Zoom prayer meeting

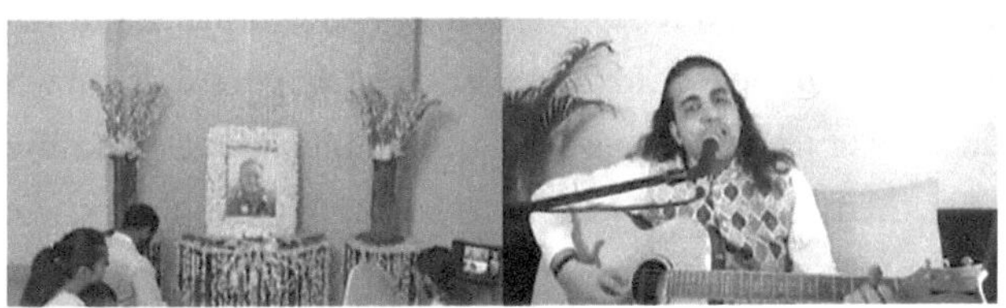

10

Celebrating Dad

Legacy is not leaving something for people, it's about leaving something in people.

People with the highest status in the world are those who ask for nothing and in return give everything.

Such was my dear dad. Whenever he raised his hands, he did it to give and not to receive. Anyone who ever went to him in need always returned fulfilled. The happiness he spread was not limited to giving financial support to people. He made sure he was there when people needed emotional support too. As a daughter, one could say I am biased, but hearing from so many known and unknown people about dad in these past six months has been an overwhelming experience and has certainly confirmed my opinion of dad. I never thought he could touch so many lives with his gestures and deeds. Some might remember his favours and some might forget, some might come back to repay the kindness and some might never return, but dad never did any of it to be recognised. Even when he had fewer resources, his heart was as open and welcoming as it was when he had a lot more to share. My daughter's words clearly put how generous my dad was: "With *nanu* around, one would never get to take out money from one's wallet as he would jump ahead of all to pay." He never did this to show off his wealth, but because it actually gave him joy to be the giver, the head, the boss.

Hearing similar stories of generosity and kindness from his family and friends and even from so many unknown people made me wonder if he was even meant for this world, a world which is so selfish and tends to forget so quickly and conveniently. But, I always tell myself that good karma can never be forgotten, and it will come back to you in double folds. Life is an echo; what you send out comes back; what you sow, you reap; what you give is what you get; and what you see in others, exists in you.

He always saw the good in others and wanted to give back in kind. In the journey of life, many may forget him and move on but some shall always remember him for he had truly touched their souls.

I am sharing some extracts from the various messages that poured from all over the world for dad. A few of them are messages that were posted online during his prayer meetings and some were conveyed to us over these past few months when I got to meet them. What I heard from these individuals made me realise that people could forget what you did, they could forget what you said, but people would never forget how you made them feel.

"Suresh was more than a friend, he was family. He and I shared the same room in the hostel when we were in Modern School and was lucky enough to connect after passing out from school as he welcomed me with his arms wide open and so much warmth. He was extremely important in my life. He was someone who gave away all what he ever had to everyone around him. I last spoke to him when he was in home isolation and was down with COVID, but was still very concerned for the rest of his family even then. Again, when I called he had been by then hospitalised and he definitely didn't sound well. It surely made me feel scared and worried for him. Can't believe we actually lost him … will miss you my dear friend."

– Rupinder Puri

(Friend from Modern school)

"I lost touch with Suresh after school and only reconnected 30 years later. And since then, every time I came to India, I would message him. I made some beautiful memories by simply talking to him. He was the richest of all who touched so many lives and I know wherever he is today be will be making new friends there too."

– Sanjay Mittal

(Batchmate from school)

"I met Suresh after almost 25 years of passing from school. He was like my *dost*, my brother! He helped me with my gymkhana elections and even helped me get a perfect chief guest for one of my events. Once, I offered to pay for something in his presence and he turned back and said, "You might be a big officer but you better not show this wallet when I am around." Such was my super sweet and caring, helpful friend."

– Sunita Trivedi

(Batchmate from school)

"Whenever I was in India, I always met him. He was available 24/7 for all of us with his super helping nature. Last time, I met him at Lodhi Hotel and had a memorable evening him accompanied by his beautiful smile and his amazing hospitality."

– Vineet Ahuja

(Batchmate from school)

"Suresh was a very helpful and friendly person. I met him at St. Stephen's College for my daughter's admission twenty years ago. He immediately took me to meet the head of department of Economics (the course my daughter had applied for) and made it all so easy and smooth for me, even without me asking him to do this for me. He would even at times happily force his help on those he truly cared for. Once when I was in Delhi and told him to meet me, he called me over to his office as he wanted me to meet someone very special. As I sat in his office he suddenly walked in the cabin holding our school headmaster Mr. A K Chaturvedi's hand; he had joined Suresh after retiring from school. It amazed me that Suresh gave sir not only a big support but also a life of dignity and respect. That day my respect for my friend increased manifold. He was a wonderful person who will always be missed by all. I will always cherish the beautiful time spent in the hostel with him and will never forget him."

– **Ravindra Gupta**

(Batchmate from school)

"My association with Suresh was 60 years old. He was a self-made man, was a true giver and full of absolute generosity. He came from a humble background and throughout studied on government scholarship. We both came from families that were not very well-off, but regardless, he created a complete empire of his own. He was the first successful businessman in his family and he ruled the world of fumigation. He created the biggest network of his friends from school and college, hats off to him for all the efforts. I will always remember him with so much pride and love. He was everyone's biggest support and always helped everyone. He will be missed by all so much."

– **Deepak Sethi**

(Batchmate from school)

"To me, Suresh was like Hanuman (a Hindu god). He was as brave and large-hearted like him! He was so pure that one could never imagine a single blemish or fault in him. He was always ready to help and was so caring, just so larger than life and giving! His heart had so much love and care for everyone. During our college days, Suresh once came to my college

Miranda House for an audition. I was surprised to see his infectious energy and was always high in spirits. He used to make everyone laugh so much and for the first time I saw his artistic side too. Years later, now he lived very close to my house and I would often see him walking and being super punctual about his routine. I feel sad I didn't get to catch up more with him while he was around. I felt that he used to fly, not walk, always moving like wind, so energetic and full of life. And I always felt his mind ran even faster than him; he was always so fast and quick. I wondered where did he get so much energy from!"

– **Maya**

(Batchmate from school)

"Suresh was special, my buddy from school days. Not only was he a very nice soul and a very nice human being, who was very close to my heart and who touched so many hearts with his behaviour, but he was also a step ahead when it came to helping anyone. There have been and will be very few and rare people like him. One could never catch him in a single frame. He brought so many of us together and will forever remain in my heart."

– **Mayank Jain**

(Batchmate from school)

"A super dildaar aadmi, he was a true yaaron ka yaar, someone who would even give his life for his friends and family. Such was my friend. He was someone who would belong to everyone. On one occasion, he came to visit me for some consultation and the moment I got a bit distracted, he quietly kept the fee in my drawer and left without making it any obvious as he knew I would have never taken it from him. Such was my friend, he will always be so badly missed."

– Dr. Vikram Jain

(Batchmate from school)

"Suresh was our SUN, and we, his friends, were like planets revolving around him. I feel blessed to say I was amongst the closest of the all planets! He was not my friend, he was my brother! He was always there whenever anyone needed him. He was everyone's, and lived for everyone's happiness. He was a rare human being. I met him on 24 July 1961 when I joined Modern School, and was in boarding house with him since I was eight years old. Since the day we met, he tightly held my hand until he took his last breath. A few weeks before he left, I myself was unwell and needed to get a few tests done. In those days home testing wasn't happening. The moment I told Suresh, he immediately called a few people and got it arranged for me in 15 minutes. Later, when I was in the ICU, still he gave me so much relief in the time of distress. Little did I know, it was my dear friend's last kind gesture towards me like so many more that he always showed towards me in all those years. He was a merit scholarship holder and he even instituted medals in Modern School and at Stephen's in the memory of his father. He was a self-made man who respected human values. I will miss my true dost till my last breath, till I meet him next. Until then, we all should celebrate an exceptional life which will not be witnessed for years to come."

– Shubhabrata Bhattacharya

(Close friend from school)

"Suresh was a great human being with even greater values. Today, to even talk about him in the past tense feels so heavy. We both belonged to the same era, went to same school, college and FMS. Had common sports interest in athletics and hockey. We had different levels of interactions over the years. He was a perfect boarding house prefect. I always wondered how the small-built Suresh managed the perfect balance between the extremely diverse groups of students from the most naughty ones to the dashing and dapper ones and studious ones! His was the toughest job and how well he would excel in it. I wondered what worked for him? The super friendly Suresh always managed to bridge the gap and maintain the balance so well. Suresh succeeded among all with his good old charm. After that I met Suresh again at the MSOSA AGM. He was different, he came well prepared and threw many questions at the president about issues and accounts. Finally, Mr. Kapur saved the day for the president. He was a firebrand and later went on to become the secretory of MSOSA. Years later, I met him again, this time he had sobered down and was an elder statesman. The generous person him was actively involved in sponsoring many events, awards and students. As I took over as the president of MSOSA in 2021 our interactions increased. He was always the first to come forward and help. Our last interaction was on 2 May, regarding helping and funding teachers. He was the first to say yes! A few days later we lost him. People like Suresh can never leave; they continue to live in our hearts forever."

– **Sunder Hemrajani**

(Went to the same school and college)

"My dear friend was the best amongst the dying breed of great gentleman. He had a heart of gold."

– **Pradeep Dinodia**

(Went to the same school)

"Suresh was blessed with an extraordinary personality. He was a pure and honest soul. He was born with a large heart and was always ready to help anyone who came in touch with him."

– **Vineet Sarin**

(Junior from school)

"Suresh was an outstanding human being. He was always known for his generosity and huge network of so many school and college friends. He was known to my family for almost 50 years, and I have so many memories with him to look back on so fondly and I shall cherish them forever. He was a great companion to the society at large."

– **Mohan Menon**

(Went to same school and college)

"Suresh was a super wonderful friend and a school mate. He brought everyone together. Our camaraderie carried on for 50 long years. He left a void that can never be filled by anyone. He will be deeply missed by all."

– **Dr. Sirinder Jit Gupta**

(Friend from school)

Suresh left a very deep mark on all his friends and associates that he made in different stages of his life. His smiling face and pleasant personality made him stand out always. I am still in disbelief that he is no longer with us now. I can never forget his readiness to help me when I hesitantly approached him a few years back, regardless of not having been able to keep in touch with him since so many years. He got so offended with my hesitation and came forward with so much warmth and cheer. He will always be remembered for years and years to come for being such a good soul, not just for his attainments which are also legendary, as an entrepreneur who rose above the ordinary

– **Sourabh Kumar**

(School friend 1966 batch)

Suresh was ever so smiling, cheerful and helpful, always bringing people together, you will be sorely missed my dear friend. You have left a huge gaping vacuum in our college lunch group

– **Ashok sajjanhar**

(College friend)

Suresh has left behind a numbness, a silence that remains so that loud that we all become deaf, he was his college lunch group's biggest strength always

– Dr. Navina Jafa

(College friend)

Feels so devasted to have lost Suresh. He was a big reason of keeping this college group so together. Ever so gracious. He will be missed deeply by all

– Jyoti sagar

(College friend)

Had known Suresh since school days, there could not have been a more sincere, affectionate and wonderful friend. He'll be badly missed

– Durgesh Shankar

(School and college friend)

The most enthusiastic of all, always willing to reach out and help whenever needed by anyone, lost a true gem

–Arvind wable

(College friend)

What a wonderful, ever so positive and smiling friend. Sad the first one to go so early like this. He will be missed by all

–Satya Sheel

(College friend)

Always the first one to send timely reminders for anything ever related to college. I will badly miss our frequent tea sessions. He was very special to me

– Sameer Sharma

(College friend)

He was such a nice and kind soul. Always ready to help and advice juniors like us. It feels like we lost a great mentor and guide.

–Parul soni

(College friend)

This was surely a big loss. One of the most gentle and kind human being. The most enthusiastic person of all our college lunches, always reminding most of us for the same and always present for each get together

–KV Eapan

(College friend)

Suresh was ever so smiling, a proud Modernite And a stephanian he always went out of his way to help anyone whoever approached him. He will be badly missed by all and by MSOSA especially

–Ashwajit Singh

(School friend)

My dear Suresh was so large hearted. Ever so smiling and full of life. No one could have ever believed that one day he will leave so quietly and suddenly. I have such beautiful memories being a part of the friends colony walking gang, he was my buddy always telling me interesting stories about his school and college, updating me about his trips and fun lunches. But what always caught my attention was his extreme dedication to his family. Whenever I would force him for breakfast after our walk he would never agree as he said that it was his time with his wife anju and if we ever told him to join us on weekends he would politely refuse saying it was his time with his grandchildren. There hasn't been a single day since I haven't missed my friend and everyday I pray that he is beautiful soul forever rests in peace.

– Madhu Bhatia

(Park Friend)

Suresh was one year senior to me in school and my hockey partner, years later we ended up becoming walking partners when he shifted to new friends colony. He used to happily come towards my side of the colony so that we could chat and walk together. Even though in the last few years he was not in the best of his health but nothing could ever take away his positivity and his beautiful smile. I will never be able to forget that most unfortunate date of 12th may 2021 when I suddenly called on his mobile at 7:30 am just to check on him how he was doing as we had not met for our walks for a very long time due to covid. To my biggest an unknown person answered his phone that day, when I asked who it was the lady on the other line said that she was his doctor and next to her on the bed was my dear friend Suresh who was no more. It gives me so much pain that someone like him was all alone in the hospital in those most challenging times when the family wasn't allowed to be with him. He will always be missed

– Pradeep Dinodia

(School Friend)

"Suresh uncle was special. I will always remember him for the guidance and mentoring on the basic principles of entrepreneurship. His life was an inspiration to many and I'm sure wherever he will be today, he will continue to spread happiness everywhere."

– Anonymous

"My friend was never seen without a smile. He was a complete *yaaron ka yaar*, a self-made entrepreneur and a dreamer. His popularity was immense. He had the ability to forge long-term friendships and was always attached to his *alma mater*. He had a sharp twinkle in his eyes. He was a good student, great alumni, a doting father and a loving husband. I will remember him for his infectious smile. There was so much warmth in his hugs. He always organised so many get-togethers, lunches and dinners for his school and college friends. His outreach was tremendous. And to prove his love for his *alma mater*, he even got both his kids admitted to the same school and college. He was a super successful businessman. Many of us shall now miss our college lunches as there would be no Suresh Gupta to give us morning reminders now! We all have to go one day, but when you lose someone as special as Suresh, the loss feels bigger. I am sure wherever he is today he will be smiling forever."

– C K Mishra

(College friend)

"Suresh was a big *yaaron ka yaar*, with a childlike enthusiasm. He would bond with everyone. He was a self-made man who got what he truly deserved. I remember when his name wasn't considered for prefect for hostel, he made a full team of friends and went to the principal and fought for what he deserved and left with his prefect badge, which he was totally worthy of, and he did his duties with utmost sincerity. He got the full batch together even before he left. He was a super restless soul for whom I can never say rest in peace as I know he never will. He will be making new friends even up in heaven!"

– Vinod Taneja

(School friend)

"Suresh uncle was just so amazing. Once I bumped into him at a restaurant, he greeted me with so much warmth and affection. When I asked for my bill, the waiter said it had already been paid. To my surprise, when I asked him who had paid the bill, he pointed towards Suresh uncle. When I told uncle this wasn't needed, he just smiled and said, 'If Divya was here I would have done the same.'"

– Anonymous

"Suresh was always so warm and loving. I remember attending his daughter's wedding and even there he was trying to make his friends so well looked after and comfortable. In fact, I even told him to go and be with other guests as it was a big event and he should be around all of them and not only his friends, yet he made all us feel so special."

– Anita Rampal

(School Friend)

"Dear Suresh was a lovable, kind-hearted and helpful member of our family. We are still not able to believe that he is no more with us. God, please give us strength to bear his loss. Om Shanti."

– Sister-in-law

"Your passing away made me lose a very dear friend. I will miss your advices on religious beliefs and occasions, our regular heart-to-heart chats and your occasional frustrations. Your keen involvement in anything that ever needed immediate assistance was remarkable. There could be nobody who would ever come close to whatever you achieved for yourself, your family, for the community and for the people around you. May God always bless a soul like you."

– Vineet Ahuja

(School Friend)

"Once I went up to Suresh bhai for some help and he immediately called for a cheque and wrote it in my name. He didn't ask any questions, neither gave any deadlines … He will be badly missed by all."

– Anonymous

"He was indeed a beacon of light and positivity. He illuminated every life he ever touched. He'll always be a part of our memories."

– Prateek Sharma

(Family friend)

"There was always something very special and very forthright about Suresh. He had an old-world charm. He was always so full of love, always ready to help, enjoy, entertain and make everyone around him happy. He was always ready to be a part of your life. he never ever asked for a favour. He was an amazing personality who shall be deeply missed and remembered by so many."

– Raghav Chandra

(College friend)

"Dear Suresh was a true all-rounder and a loveable human being who was extremely helpful and kind to all who sought his help. He was a tower of strength for our entire family. As his elder brother, I am justifiably proud of him and miss him immensely. It's impossible to get an affectionate and loving brother like him ever. We all miss him so much. This loss can never be compensated. May God bless him and give us the strength to bear this irreparable loss. Om Shanti."

– Brother

"Suresh was so special that even when he is not amongst us today, I can still feel his presence everywhere. He might have left us in physical form, but he is definitely a part of this reunion in school today in full spirit. In fact, the day this idea of the reunion came up, my first thought was how can it be possible without our very dear Suresh. He was the one who would always push and motivate us. He always got all of us together. It's sad we lost our dear friend so soon and so suddenly."

– Deepak Bhandari

(School friend)

"Divya, your father was the most wonderful man we had the privilege of knowing. Even though he's no longer on this earth, his laughter and his spirit will be with us forever."

– Anonymous

"Every year, I used to look forward to receiving my Diwali wishes from Suresh! Not that I used to wait for the gift, but I used to wait for that glass of drink with my dear friend as no matter what, he would never miss an opportunity to meet his old friends. And what better occasion than Diwali! This Diwali I missed him so much and I am sure many more like me would have missed his yearly tradition so much."

– Anonymous

"Many years after passing from school, one day I bumped into Suresh. He came from behind and caught me hard. I was surprised how he had recognised me after so many years. I even joked that it was due to the three circles I had at the back of my head that made me a bit unique for him to remember me. But he anyways had a very sharp memory. He asked me something about school and I told him I was hardly a Modernite as I had studied there for a very few years. Suresh got angry and told me always remember once a Modernite, always a Modernite. Since that day all because of him, I got back to my school and my old friends, and here I am today attending my fiftieth reunion only because of my dear friend Suresh!"

– Ambuj Gupta

(School friend)

"I had known Suresh for a very long time. We all remember him as large-hearted and a giver, but I also saw a very different side of his personality that I can never forget. Suresh was at that time newly married and he had come to the railway station to drop his wife Anju, who was going to Kanpur. As the train began to move, Suresh began to run after it as a matter of love and concern for his wife. I cannot forget that romantic side that I am sure not many knew of. DDLJ came years later, but I saw it that day!"

– **Sameer Mathur**

(School friend)

"I understand the pain of losing father. Although I have not met him, but his reflection is there in you which clearly depicts how nice he was. I am sure great people like him are always doing good where ever they are."

— **Anonymous**

"I am deeply saddened to see this. The last memory of uncle was from Sri Fort park on a Sunday afternoon. And I remember telling him that he was looking as handsome as ever. I will always remember you, Uncle."

– **Chandni Gupta**

(Family friend)

"Once I was at Lodhi Hotel dining with my family, and on the next table I saw this gentleman, so cheerful and positive. His smile just reminded me of you, Divya … and yes, it was your dad! He reminded me so much of you as soon as I saw him. Even his picture that was posted on Facebook with his obituary was so full of life and so cheerful that the loss actually felt so personal, even for those who had never met or interacted with him!"

– Anonymous

"I remember uncle as always smiling and being full of positive energy. He's gone too sudden and too soon. May his soul rest in peace and may God give you all the strength to overcome your grief and live your life the way uncle would have wanted you to."

– Anonymous

"I have no words to express our loss as a family. All of us are together in this. My angel, my father figure, my guide, my pillar, my support system, has left us. And I still can't believe it. I have a pit in my stomach. But *didi*, the person that he was, God is going to take very good care of him. He's in a happy, peaceful place, I promise you. He's protecting us from there, loving us always. Be strong, we are all with you in this. This isn't just our loss, it's a loss to humanity."

– Anonymous

"Suresh was a special friend, who often touched people with his gestures. I remember when I was asked to speak in his prayer meeting I just could not because if I had, I would have cried. I remember when we were kids and in school, it was our exam day, and I was down with high fever. Still, my parents forced me to go and take the exam in school. As I reached school, Suresh and few more were a bit unwell and were taking exam in the school sanitorium. As I was very unwell, I wasn't able to write and the time was up. The teacher forced me to submit my paper, but Suresh got up and fought on my behalf and forced the teacher to give me 30 minutes more to write and helped me so much that day. I shall never be able to forget this gesture in my life, even after so many years of passing out from school. He was a selfless man, someone who would only give and never ask favours! Once he visited one of my hotel properties and stayed there and later told me that he had visited, upon which I got upset that why he didn't tell me before, I would have got him a royal treatment and a better deal. But I know that's why he didn't tell me as he could never take favours! I miss my friend so much."

– **Pradeep Jain**

(School friend)

"Suresh was the only one who would hold the whole batch together, push everyone and motivate everyone to come together and stay connected. Not everyone can make so much effort as he always did for his friends. I was poor at replying back to messages in the batch message group and would often miss many. Immediately, Suresh would message me personally and push me to reply and confirm if it was needed. His personal calls and that push will always be missed so badly by all of us."

– **Anonymous**

"Divya, today when I saw uncle's prayer meeting, I regretted missing the opportunity to meet someone like him. The way everyone spoke about him not only said what an amazing human being he was but also showed how much he was loved by so many. I felt terrible for not meeting him ever."

– Anonymous

"Last I spoke to him, he was in the hospital and was COVID-positive. Still, he was trying to be hopeful and concerned about others as much as he could in that situation. I had never imagined my friend would leave me just a few days after that … a big loss."

– Anonymous

"Suresh was special, a short and tiny guy of our batch. I fondly remember the transistor episode with him where he got in trouble, but what I also remember of him is that he would never give up! He used to participate in all races and used to run to the best of his capacity till he would win, and just after crossing the finishing line, he would just collapse. He would always give his best to anything he would be a part of. He was always so helpful and nice."

– Ashok Nayyar

(School friend)

"I know no words are enough to console you, Divya. I came to know yesterday while attending the Zoom prayer meet how loving and inspiring your father was. People like him live forever in everyone's heart."

– Anonymous

Suresh uncle was not only helpful, he was also very pure. Once, as one of his neighbours, I requested him to become the guarantor for my passport verification. The officer went to his office and questioned uncle that why he was doing it. Did he actually know me? To which, uncle lovingly replied "*Arre* he is like my son. I can blindly take his guarantee." Our interactions were very limited, and he didn't actually need to do that for me. It felt so nice that this world still had people like him. Losing him felt such a personal loss.

– Neighbour

Even after months of losing him just yesterday when I heard Suresh's name from a Friend it brought back so many memories of our beautiful times together in school and college,he was my senior and what an amazing one at it ..a guide, a mentor in every true sense.always with a beautiful smile that I still

Miss so much.i was in the hostel with him and he always managed things so beautifully.sometimes I felt his veins didn't have blood, it just had endless love for his school and college. always ready to help and serve his institutes however he could. what he did for our heardmaster

Mr. Chaturvedi was commendable, I remember Everytime I met sir after his retirement he would be full of so much love and praise for Suresh. the void Suresh left behind can never be filled by anyone, even today how he left leaves behind so much sadness, but he will be celebrated soon and we all will be a part of it .

– SD Mudgil

(Junior from school and college)

"Suresh bhai was my senior, and this seniority was always maintained. He was someone with immense commitment and great communication skills. He had great organising abilities. At college lunches, he was always the first one to reach and would push others too and was forever ready with a helping hand for all. He was a self-made man with a forever smiling face. He was not someone who would seek any limelight. In fact, he always earned it through his humility and goodness. For me and for many others, he was a model student as described by our then principal Mr. M N Kapur. He carried forward the legacy as he excelled in every field and followed the school motto to the tee. He was a model Modernite and a model Stephanian. In school, we had the same house Lajpat, and our house master was Mr. A K Chaturvedi. The loyal and ideal student that Suresh bhai was he continued to seek sir's blessings even after he retired from school and made him join his business with full respect and honour. He was a successful entrepreneur of 1970s; he had pushed away job opportunities and gained so much success in his business venture. He contributed to the society immensely. This was surely no time and age for him to go. It feels like the sun set too soon and too early for him! Maybe someone like him was more wanted by God up there. He will be deeply missed forever."

– Justice Sanjay Krishan Kaul
(Chairman Modernites Trust)

Suresh was my brother and truest friend in every regard. He was always there, supporting me through all my ups and downs.his loss has left a void forever which nobody can ever fill. He will always stay in my heart and will be remembered and cherished forever!

Chu lete hai tere ahsaas ko,band ankhoonse bhi,tujhe mehsoos karne ke liye,tu samne ho,zaroori nahi!

– Sunil Malhotra
(Close friend)

Suresh and I were batchmates of economics hons (1970-73) at St Stephens collage delhi. Our middleclass backgrounds brought us closer and in those 3 years, he became my closest college friend. After graduation, we both chose to be first generation entrepreneurs and took up entirely different areas of work that made us very busy in our respective worlds with intermittent communications for many years. Suresh excelled in his field and was always very hardworking, focused, dedicated and strong. He achieved most of his goals with his great communication skills, friendly nature and honesty. He was a very dependable friend who believed in long lasting friendships. In my personal experience, he stood by me through thick and thin like a solid rock in the time of need. For years we remained occupied in our respective careers and families but surprisingly lockdown got us back together after years to once again renew old memories and revisit the past journey of the last 50+ years. Till his last days we were in touch and it was a big shock to lose him like a shooting star within a span of few days after he got covid positive. Till date I have not been able to reconcile with the reality of his untimely and tragic demise.

Dear Suresh, you will always be missed and will remain in my heart forever.

– **Kuldip Rathi**
(College friend)

"I miss you so much, *nanu* … I still can't accept the fact that you are no longer with us. I miss hugging you, coming to get your advice, going for coffees and lunches with you and a list of endless other things I used to enjoy with you. I hope that one day I will be able to hug you like I used to and see that ever so shining smile again. You were amazing, and I know that you still are. I keep remembering you through happy and sad moments of life, and I'd give anything to get you back. I will cherish all those amazing memories God gave me with you, but I wish I could have got more. You were, and always will be, the best *nanu* I could have ever asked for. Love you always and forever."

– **Manya**
(Granddaughter)

Spend time with those who matter, one of the days we will say either.

"We wish we had or we're glad we did."

Dad with mom and manya

School 1970 batchmates

Dad with his school friends

Dad with his dear friend Mr CK Mishra

Dad with his dear friend Mr Amitabh Kant

Dad with his college lunch group

Dad with his family

11

The New Me

Loss has changed the way I view life now. Nothing feels the same or will be the same ever again. People say time heals everything, but I feel it only teaches you to live with pain for the rest of your life. Overnight, something changed. Just imagining the pain of never being able to see my father ever again broke something inside me, and every time I revisited that day of loss, it broke me further.

I must admit writing this book brought a bag of extremely mixed feelings. It brought me closer to dad. Every beautiful memory associated with him got a smile on my face; every experience that I shared made me realise how lucky I was to be his daughter. As I dwelled more and more on the past, it filled me with so much gratitude for the years he had spent in my life. This book made me realise that earlier he was near yet so far; I had to go and meet him, call and speak to him and wait to be with him, but now he was so far and yet so near! To be with him now all I needed was to close my eyes and think of him and look at his picture and share my feelings with him. I could take him anywhere and everywhere in my heart. Many of my friends even told me that now my dear dad was my guarding angel, someone who was always up there to protect me and shower me with his love and blessings, someone who would now even request God to get my wishes granted even sooner than before. In a way, he was the direct link with the divine power now.

It made me wonder how badly I missed his physical presence in my life after I got married. I would often crib about it, and however strange it may sound, but dad made sure he left addressing my biggest complaint by not only spending his most crucial last few days only and only with me but also giving me the whole idea of writing this book after he had left. Now, I could directly form a connection with him that no one in this world could break or take away from me. But on the other hand, writing was also one of the most painful decisions to take. Just the thought of loss of a parent makes one cry, even the mention of it brings tear to one's eyes every time, and here I was revisiting those dreadful days again and again as I was writing one chapter after another. Every time I wrote about the pain that dad went though as a COVID patient, it left me heartbroken.

It also made me face the most shocking reality of life that until the pain is not personal, it never hurts! Not that I would ever want anyone to experience what many of us went through during the second wave, but one surely cannot feel the intensity of the pain until they actually get to feel it themselves. When I saw so many people around me completely unaffected or not bothered initially, it made me angry. But slowly I realised everyone has their own journey; no one can take the road that's meant for you, and hence, no one can share the happiness and pain that's written in your destiny. Everything is about the divine time and karmic balance that one has to settle for in one's present life. We are no one to decide about our fate no matter how hard we may try. And that's when I decided to forgive and forget those who didn't deserve the attention in my life now, surprisingly forgiveness came easy to me for the first time ever in so many years. I guess TIME has a wonderful way of showing us what really matters!

Life had taken a new meaning for me since my dad's death. I was not the same person I was before he died. It was almost impossible to explain to friends and family all the ways that I had changed. The friends and family who had stood by me saw who I had now become and gave me the space to evolve. The friends and family who expected me to remain unchanged by loss were no longer a significant part of my life. I needed to make my inner circle small to heal and move forward. Did anyone else experienced this too? Was this the right way to feel and react I often ask myself even today.

The most important lesson I ever learnt and decided to follow for the rest of my life was priorities! For the first time ever, I realised that if we aren't someone's priority, there is no point being in their life and keeping them in ours. But that doesn't mean we must cut them off or fight with them; we must simply learn to ignore them and move on and make them the most insignificant part of our existence. And maybe when tomorrow they go through a similar experience just watch them silently. I always made extra efforts to hold on to old and new relationships close to my heart and maintain them as much as I could to the best of my capacity, another teaching from dad, which I felt it was time to let go of!

Death is the biggest loss in one's life and teaches you lessons for a lifetime. During the pandemic as we mourned in isolation, it was a very lonely time, a time when you needed that tight hug of concern the most. Everyone feared they would catch the deadly virus, and hence, were forced to maintain a distance. As I spent that time all alone weeping, I also got time to think a lot about life and the people in it. It was during this time that I realised even the smallest gestures from friends and family left a deep impact on my mind. Every word mattered and every action affected. Initially, the phone rang non-stop, but for days I didn't wanted to talk to anyone at all. Every call would, eventually, leave me sobbing for hours, and it was taking a toll on my health and mind. I did not just close the doors of my house for anyone to meet me, I also closed the doors of my heart for anyone at all! Only the immediate family of my husband Manish and my daughter Manya were my biggest support and only shoulders to cry on. It was during this time that a few special people forced themselves into my life, in my sad and dark space and touched my life for a lifetime. They were those for whom my tears mattered; unable to handle my silence, they just wanted me to be normal again, be myself again!

The new me was different. I was once a party person, full of life, always ready to have fun and enjoy. I was the famous selfie queen as per most of my friends, but not anymore. One day could change me so much that at times it still feels strange. I had suddenly forgotten to smile and had begun to hate social media, which was once my life. I used to freely share my life with everyone, but not anymore. I just didn't feel normal at all; it felt like my heart had just left my soul. And the biggest question that I asked myself so many times was, "WHY ME?" It hit me so hard that I wondered why God chose me to be in this place when I had always maintained a happy and beautiful relationship with God. How could he put me through so much pain? I almost felt I was losing my divine connection with God with each passing day.

Time also reminded me of dad's biggest teaching again and again: stand by people in their sad times, even if you miss their happy days! Although I had always made sure I did the same, unfortunately, it was my time to experience it myself and set my future goals. It was time to differentiate between friends of convenience and friends of concern! As I write this, I want to take the opportunity for the first time to extend my heartfelt gratitude for every friend, family and well-wishers who stood by me in the time of need and helped me heal so much. Maybe it wasn't the right time to thank as I wasn't able to feel it then, but every time someone called, sent a heartfelt message that I was on their mind, sent food and flowers to make me feel better and, most importantly, every time someone made an effort to visit me, it touched my heart and left a deep impact on my mind. And even a bigger thank you to all those who didn't do any of it! It helped me see the real them and where I stood on their priority list. Instead of being upset, I felt relieved from the burden of so many unwanted friendships and relationships that I was holding on to so close to my heart till now. It brought an end to so many family bonds that weren't serving their purpose anyways, but I had been holding on to them because of societal pressure. It just somehow felt that dad ended all this for me so I could move on in life uninterrupted. As bad as it may sound, I felt free and relieved. Suddenly, what one would think or say just didn't matter anymore. As days turned into weeks and weeks into months, I remained home, isolated and completely disconnected from the world outside that was once my life, as a happening social butterfly!

The first time I stepped out, I remember was when I had to go and take my vaccination shot. There, I saw a lady in her early 60s who had brought her 90-year-old father for his second dose of vaccination. It hit me so badly; here I was not even 40 and had lost my dad so young. I did not even get the opportunity to serve him the way he did for all of us. Why as kids were we so unfortunate that God didn't even give us a chance to look after our dad when he needed us the most? Why did he have to go through this pain all alone? This horrible feeling left me with a throbbing pain once again! Strangely enough, seeing elderly people made me so sad; it made me realise that we weren't the lucky ones to have that age group around us to serve them and protect them when they needed us the most. It felt sad that I was not lucky enough to get the opportunity to serve him in his old age in this lifetime. I asked, "Dad, what was the rush?" Dad was like a small kid who needed a lot of love and nurturing, especially when he was unwell. He used to like everyone to be around him, talk to him, comfort him. How he must have felt when he was in the hospital left to deal with everything alone? But having said that, his biggest wish was not being dependent on anyone in his old age. He used to say that he would never want to be bedridden in any circumstance or be dependent on others. I guess as he was God's loved child, God heard his wish first and not mine! Just the other day, I heard a very strange thing. Someone told me that when the soul is ready to leave the body in their last moments, the journey further becomes harder and more painful if they have their loved ones around them.

Strangely enough, my dad was alone even during this most crucial time and left alone, hopefully, without this unbearable pain of seeing us all grieving for him. Once again, it made me feel that he was really loved by God! He surely was special.

Moving back in the selfish world wasn't easy; it almost took me 7 months to make my first public appearance. It was like living a nightmare every time I met someone. It amazed me that every time I gathered courage to step out after a lot of resistance, someone would walk up to me to pay their condolences! It broke me so badly and surprised me that if they didn't have time to do it for so long, had no time for one message or phone call, then why do they even bother to do it now and make me feel more miserable and uncomfortable. Having said that, I also experienced pure love from so many around me. I remember I had gone to a particular place and this friend gave me the tightest hug for a good five minutes. The warmth of her genuine love was so strong that not a word was exchanged and yet I felt so much better and so loved. My heart searched for a place where I didn't have to pretend to be normal. I could be happy, then sad and then maybe, happy again. To all those who haven't felt this pain, all I can say is when you invite a grieving person somewhere, let them know that their grief is invited too. Just let them be themselves.

Sometimes, it so happens that we say a lot that doesn't make sense, and sometimes, we don't say anything at all but it leaves such a deep impact on our hearts! Sometimes, those endless phone calls didn't make any sense but a single message touched my feelings so strongly. This time also brought me closer to friends who shared the same pain; like me they had also lost a loved one in the past. It was the time to bond over emotions and have a heart-to-heart connect. I shall now treasure these relationships for a lifetime. The most beautiful feeling is to hold someone's hand through their grief, especially if you have experienced it yourself; it can be one's biggest purpose in life, and I felt blessed to find a few friends who just did that for me. I know they are reading this today, so I want to thank them from the bottom of my heart and let them know they will always hold the most special place in my life. Talking about sharing pain, I too for the first time felt my husband's pain six years after he lost his dad. That time I had felt bad for him, was shattered to see him cry and was with him in his sorrow, but only after I lost my own father did I feel what he had gone through when he had lost his dad at such a young age. I felt so bad for him that I was actually at a loss for words. During his worst time, I acted as his biggest strength, pushed him to come out of his grief and helped him get back to work. But today, here I was lost and broken, totally unaffected when Manish said how helpless he was to see me in my grief and unable to pull me out the way I had done for him, I guess everyone has a different way to mourn a personal loss.

The people you will always remember are the ones who made you feel loved at your lowest! My most precious relationship was lost, but I found some genuine ones that I'll make sure I keep close to my heart as long as I live. They shared my pain when I needed them the most. They forced me for coffee and outings and made efforts to normalise my life as much as they could. After almost seven months now, even today when I step out, there is always something missing; every event looks incomplete and makes me feel so lost and alone even in the biggest gathering. My eyes constantly search for dad in every person I meet, but I guess it is just the beginning of missing him for the rest of my life, something that I will now have to live with forever!

When you experience loss people say you will move though 5 stages of grief…denial, anger, bargaining, depression and acceptance… But what they didn't tell was that you'll cycle through them all every day!

My grief compelled me to seek counselling. It was suggest by a friend who had gone through the same emotions and felt I wasn't coping up fine. As I began my grief sessions, there was an outburst of emotions, so much fear, anger, guilt and pain trapped in my heart, all that was making me sink day by day. My sessions gave my emotions a window. The counsellor was a beautiful soul who heard me every day cry and waited for me to, eventually, talk. There was so much to tell and ask. Since dad got unwell, I had held back so much inside me, thinking that once he would be oaky, it would get back to normal. But when it didn't happen that was when my feelings got badly suppressed. It took me back to those last 12 days when I was a changed person, deprived of sleep, support, guidance and mental peace. So much so that I didn't even know what I was eating; I had not even combed my hair for days. Whether those sessions helped, I don't know, but they did make me feel very light after a few days. The finale was a divine door session where they would help you connect with the departed soul once. Just the thought of it both excited me and disturbed me. On the one hand, I wanted to meet dad, ask him how he was and whether he was angry with me, and on the other hand, I didn't know how I would handle it. I wondered if it would be okay to disturb him. On the day of the session, I got so overwhelmed with emotions and cried so much that I could not create a direct connection with dad, but later, the third medium did answer a few questions that were on my mind, and it did give me a bit of relief and helped me calm down.

People cry not because they are weak, but because they've been strong for too long.

But having said that, being in a long period of grief or being so emotionally drained for such a long time didn't make me weak. My tears didn't mean I needed help or needed to be supported. It's just my way of dealing with my grief. Maybe I had a very strong and dominating emotional side or had lesser control over my feelings unlike someone else in a similar situation. Any form of detachment has always troubled me and taken very long to settle. Even when the first ever detachment happened in my life when I lost my grandfather (Nana) when I was very young. I was very close to him being the first grandchild in the family, always received a lot of love and affection from him. Losing him made me so sad and heartbroken that I almost stopped visiting my mom's maternal side of home in Kanpur after his demise. Then when I got married, it was so tough to accept this big change in my life. Leaving behind my house, my room, my comfort zone and my family was unbearable for a long time and settling in a huge joint family was even tougher. I was so lost and confused! The next was when I lost my father-in-law. Although we shared a very formal relationship, losing him wasn't easy. Just the thought of being unable to see him ever again and not have him around was so unimaginable and uncomfortable. Living with someone and then one fine day having to accept the fact that they won't be around ever again is so painful at times you run short of words to actually explain how you are feeling in that moment. His demise also created an emptiness not only in our house, but also in our lives that remains even today, mostly unsaid and unexplained.

And now that I have experienced one of the biggest separation of my life from my own father, it surely had to be the toughest. We, as adults, know that if one has taken birth, they will eventually leave for a better world. I remember we would often get into conversations with friends in the same age group about aging parents that it's so tough to deal with this sinking feeling that one fine day we would lose them as no one could live forever. But believe me, when it actually happens and you get to face it, and no matter how well you have prepared yourself for the worst, it all just comes crashing down. Your reactions, your feelings and your burst of emotions is beyond control and unexplainable.

Life will surely move ahead. Even after a loss, we will learn to live again, smile again and slowly get back to the routine, but the excruciating pain to see your other parent all alone, dealing with the loss and learning to live without their soulmate will make this wound fresh every day. When you lose one parent, you get to see the other parent suffer even more. I lost my father, but losing a husband of 42 years was even a bigger loss for my mother. She had dedicated her whole life to my dad, his house and their family! And to now see her learn to live each day without him looked so traumatic and unimaginable. They were like the two ends of a rope, so different in temperament and nature, yet with one main and common priority that was family. They lived selflessly, asking nothing at all in return and wishing only to see us happy and settled. I guess most parents are like that. Mine weren't different, but for me the most special one always!

This new me taught me that life was vulnerable and unexpected. All our life, we wait for one right time, one perfect moment, and sometimes, it never comes. Regardless of having had the most simple and giving parents, I feel so helpless for being unable to do anything at all for them. They always prioritised us and overlooked their own happiness and joy. So many of their dreams remained unfulfilled, so many tasks undone and so many words unsaid. Dad always wanted to get the family together and travel together. Just a few months back, he had told mom that for his milestone birthday, he would love to take the immediate family to Goa as he wanted everyone to wear personalised t-shirts and flaunt them. Sometimes small gestures and moments make life so beautiful and memorable, then why just wait? For whom?

That milestone birthday never came. Today, I wonder if one should even wait for that milestone birthday. Every birthday is special, and it must be celebrated like there is no tomorrow. There must have been so many things dad would have wanted to do and had been waiting for the right time to come, but unfortunately, that right time never came. So, live in today and enjoy it as if there is no tomorrow. It also taught me that there is no space in this world for extremely pure people. Dad was always too kind. As some of his friends said he had no blemish, no fault; he trusted people too quickly, took risks and they did not always leave him with the best results and many a times left him cheated and disheartened. Surprisingly, dad was never vocal about his feelings and never made anyone feel that he was hurt or disappointed, instead he used to be upset deep inside and kept it to himself. He never showed any hatred or discomfort towards any relationship, and today, I feel that was wrong too. It made him suffer on the inside. It also taught me not to live with grudges and always speak my heart out without caring about the outcome. No one is perfect and that's the fact of life.

This loss taught me that nothing in life is permanent and we can't hold on to anything forever. I see my mom struggle with dad's memories and break down every day. Today, she does things that dad used to like, dress up how he wanted her to and has made the changes in her life that he would have loved to see, but unfortunately, he is not there to see and it breaks my heart. It makes me wonder why we take so long to realise the importance of our loved ones in our life or only do it when they are gone. Why not when they are still around? We don't really take people for granted, but we surely delay telling them how much they mean to us and how deeply they are loved. Today, I may write hundreds of pages on my own dad, but it troubles me that I didn't really tell him how much I loved him and how proud I was of being his daughter when he was around. The right time never came.

So, to all those who are reading this, take the opportunity to tell your parents how much you love them and value their presence in your life, be good to them, treasure the days you spend with them, enjoy that special call that you receive from them, don't miss out an opportunity to meet them or travel with them, let them know that you realise what they have done for you and how proud you are of all those sacrifices and achievements, hear those lectures and suggestions that may be the best lessons for life and, most importantly, often give them that tight hug as if there is no tomorrow because one day you might realise that you can't do any of it ever again. That feeling would be unbearable, just like how I feel today! But do it only if you feel it from the heart, for relationships that have given you true love and have served you to the best of their capacity. Do it for people who truly mean something in your life and for those for whom you were always special and were their priority. Don't do anything ever under pressure; do it only if you feel it from your heart and it might bring you happiness and relief.

Today, I miss the warmth of my dad's hug, his smile every time I would tell him to pose for my selfie pictures and the feeling of extreme comfort that I used to get holding his hands. When Google maps doesn't work, I think of him; when I have to take an important decision, my heart looks for him. Just the other day, I told my mom that this book writing and publishing seems so tough for me as it's a completely new territory for me. I have no experience in it, whereas my own dad helped so many friends with their book launch numerous times, attended so many book launches and helped in promoting their books. He would often buy so many author-signed copies to gift to others that even today there are so many books kept in his office, and today, his own daughter struggles hard to find the right direction in this new field, so lost and clueless. I told mom how I wish dad was here to help me, to which she replied if dad was here I would not be writing this book at all… what followed was silence and a tear from our eyes.

Always remember, some losses are irreplaceable, but you are definitely one of those lucky ones who can delay it and live the most in the present so that no matter what tomorrow holds for you, it will surely hold less pain, unlike mine.

Make yourself the priority. At the end of the day, you are your longest commitment!

A lesson I learnt this year.

12

The Show Must Go On...

Dad is not gone; he lives on in the hearts of all who love him.

But it can be extremely exhausting to keep his memory alive in a world that is likely to move on without him, eventually. The loss of a loved one often fills the immediate family with so many emotions — shock, frustration, anger, sadness, fear, anxiety, forgetfulness and complete denial. A few months passed by and our hearts were filled with envy, loneliness, resentment, confusion, lack of faith and complete disbelief. Later, we experienced slow thinking, numerous ups and downs, continued tiredness and lack of concentration and frequent panic attacks. Anyone who has ever experienced a death of a loved one would relate to all this and more.

Moving on is the toughest part of anyone's grief. Every day one learns to live and the very next day it looks so impossible. A constant struggle to survive without one's loved one and slowly learn to breathe and live, and maybe finally, learn to hide one's tears with a smile for those who are left behind. Dad's demise changed the little daddy's girl I had always been. I never knew losing him would make me lose myself. Knowingly or unknowingly, I got so burdened with responsibility that I never realised it. It felt like growing up in just a day or maybe a few hours. How protected we all feel, especially daughters, with our fathers around! I felt the vacuum for the first time. And now all of a sudden, I had to look after mom that too in her most vulnerable phase. Every first things after a death are tough. My first Father's Day, which came immediately after he left, left me numb. I suddenly had no one to wish. My father was no more and how miserably this feeling broke me; being a fatherless daughter made me feel so alone and helpless. I remember on one occasion when my husband Manish had said something to me in a slightly loud tone, I immediately had non-stop tears rolling down my eyes as I told him that now he could scold me as my dad wasn't around and my biggest pride was gone. Although he felt very bad that I was hurt, I can now feel it wasn't due to his words that I was hurt so badly. It was because of the void that had been created in my life so suddenly that I wasn't able to handle.

Each festival that came after dad's death had now a different meaning in my life. I have always enjoyed celebrating with all rituals and festivities in place, but suddenly, every festival felt so meaningless and I was unable to perform any ritual properly. Everything had suddenly lost its joy and charm. Even though I had not celebrated Diwali with dad for years, the first Diwali without him turned out to be so terrible and distressing. I would plan for these festivals days and weeks in advance, but this time I was so lost that I could hardly manage basic rituals and could light only a few *diyas*. Somehow, the relevance of festivals had just suddenly diminished in my life.

I feel grief is like our fingerprints; it's uniquely ours and no one else can have the same one. Everyone around us has a different way of grieving, and they all have a different range of emotions. We all have our own ways and take our own time. The most awful situation for me was when someone I didn't known much would suddenly ask about dad and I would barely manage to get any words out of my mouth and fathom the courage to say that he was no more. Every time this happened, how I wished it was not true. Maybe it was just the worst nightmare of my life. It was difficult to imagine how life had changed in these past few months. Just the other day, he was with us. I had spoken to him over the phone and he had sent me a beautiful message, and today, he is gone! In fact, it was even more painful to explain the series of events of that day to people who would ask about it. To some, it may be just a story or a piece of information, but to me it was like living that torture, that pain all over again.

I had never imagined how strenuous and difficult it would be to talk about your loved ones in the past tense.

Not just occasions and festivals, but everything reminded me of him, and I felt so incomplete without his happy and cheerful presence. After almost six months of losing him, I gathered courage to travel for a short weekend break on the insistence of my family, and I promised myself that I wouldn't cry or make anyone around me uncomfortable as they too needed this break. We chose a remote location, simple and less crowded so that I could stay isolated, alone and, most importantly, undisturbed. Despite all that effort, I bumped into my dad's old friend. Although we had never met or spoken before, he started to speak about my dad so fondly and affectionately. As he spoke, the volcano of emotions inside me just erupted and I began to cry as if it was beyond control.

It reminded me that it was impossible to run away from one's emotions and, most importantly, one's grief, and I was definitely not ready to face it either. Over the next two days until we were in the resort, I tried my best to avoid that uncle as every time I saw him, he reminded me of dad. Moreover, he had come there to plan his seventieth birthday. It filled me with so much sadness wondering why my dad didn't get to celebrate any of his milestones and left with all the plans incomplete. On the day of our checkout, that uncle again walked up to me and said my smile reminded him of my dad, his dear friend, every time he saw me. "You just smile like Suresh," he said and I quietly left the resort with silent tears in my eyes and an extremely heavy heart. On our way back, I realised running away from reality could surely be delayed but could never be escaped.

Talking about escaping, it somehow felt there was something that was constantly pushing me towards dad's memories more and more, no matter how hard I tried to run away from it. The first bond has surely been this book as with it I have literally lived with dad even more than I had when he was alive. I have thought about him day and night with this book and lived every memory several times over. It was during reliving these memories I remembered something that was very close to his heart — his school's fiftieth year reunion. I remember dad had been so excited about it for two to three years. One day, I even got a little angry seeing his excitement and told him to relax and just let it happen first. I never thought that he wouldn't be able to be a part of it, eventually.

The planning for this reunion had begun in 2018; groups were formed, discussions were done and pre-reunion get-togethers had also began in 2019. My dad had happily organised a few, hosted them and sponsored them with so much love and happiness. His excitement to meet his old batchmates once again back in school was evident on his face all this while. In fact, he was instrumental in convincing so many of his overseas friends to consider coming to India just to attend this special occasion. But as God had planned, 2020, the actual year of the reunion that coincided with the school's golden jubilee year, left every Modernite disappointed. They did have a Zoom reunion where dad sang a beautiful and long poem, leaving behind a beautiful and most precious voice note for us.

Last month, I received a call from one of the MSOSA members asking me to join the organising committee for the reunion of dad's batch that was finally happening in school premises in December 2021. My very first reaction was a straight NO. This was something I had not thought I would ever do and that too without dad. I remember even in March 2021 when things were slightly better post the first COVID wave, there were talks to organise it again and that time dad was the convener of the event, and he had asked me to help him. However, the event was called off five days before it was supposed to happen as the second wave had begun. So why would I do it now when the only batchmate that the 1970 batch lost in 2021 to COVID was my Dad!

That night I cried so much, asking God why did it happen to only us in the whole batch. Why was the most enthusiastic soul lost? And I decided not to take up this responsibility as just the thought of it was already breaking me so badly. The next morning my mom told me that I had to do this, for no one else but for dad! I was amazed that she never really was a part of dad's school groups; she had hardly attended any events or bonded with any old friend. But this time, she said that not only should I do it for dad's happiness as he really wanted this reunion to happen, but she also said she would attend it and represent dad that day. It amazed and gave me so much courage to get involved in planning the event and I finally said yes!

Despite the fact that dad was so close to so many of his school friends, I had known only a few of them. So when this huge task of convincing his batchmates to attend the reunion was given to me, I found it really difficult as I hardly knew anyone, and on top of it, dad wasn't around. But I had to do this for dad! For a very strange reason, I felt this too was a sign from the universe. Just when I was feeling so lost and alone, dad sent the warmth of so many people who loved him so much. Every person I spoke to, spoke with so much fondness for him. The heaviness in their hearts of losing a dear friend was still so evident and they were happy to finally connect with me after so many years. Surprisingly, everyone had one common thing to say that this reunion wouldn't be the same without dad and how amazing he was at organising such events and pushing everyone to do the same to the best if their ability.

As the final day came close, I literally had butterflies in my stomach. Again and again, the thought of meeting dad's friends and that too in his most favourite place — his school — was giving me sleepless nights. Finally, it was 12 December, the day of the reunion and my heart felt so low. Coincidentally, it was also the seven month anniversary of dad's departure that day. It just felt life was conveying that what goes around comes around. All my life, I had stayed away from these reunions as dad was there and mom didn't attend any of them. But today, both of us were getting ready to represent him in an event that he had been obsessing over for past the two years!

I told my husband that everyone would be so happy and cheerful today meeting old friends, but mom and I would feel so empty and would be full of pain not being able to see dad amongst them. As I drove inside the school, everything reminded me of him. I remembered the childlike enthusiasm that he would display every time he entered the school. And then began one of the longest afternoons of my life. As I wore a badge with my name on it and was introduced as Mr. Suresh Gupta's daughter, there was a rain of endless hugs, conversations, touching moments and emotional outbursts from each and every friend of dad's present at the venue.

The moment they heard my name, the reactions just changed — a casual hello changed into a shower of love and affection. One by one, each friend spoke about dad with so much fondness that to hold back tears became almost impossible. That they remembered him and missed him so badly was so evident in their words. In fact, some even said that to imagine this reunion without him was almost impossible and they felt he was among them holding a glass in his hand, jumping around everywhere with his big smile. They said that dad might not be physically around, but he would always remain an integral part of the 1970 batch as he was the life and soul of this batch.

They all spoke about how dad's sudden demise had left them shocked and heartbroken. In fact, some of them even told me that dad was even in touch with them from the hospital, keeping a check on their well-being and was still concerned about his friends. So, it was tough for them to imagine that he was gone. Some even joked that they would never buy any passes for any such reunions as dad used to buy it for them and tell them that they only had to be present on the final day. This was probably the first time they were buying it and missing their friend even more. It wasn't just dad's generosity that they were missing, it was how he used to make them feel loved that they missed the most.

That day I realised that some people continue to live on even if they are gone, thanks to the beautiful memories they leave behind. Soon after mom came for the reunion, and she was welcomed with so much love that she actually turned and told me in the middle of the lunch that today she was proud to be my father's wife! All these years, mom had never attended such reunions. As a typical non-Modernite spouse, she used to get bored, but this time she was representing dad and that actually called for so much courage and strength. She also broke down on many instances, but every time someone shared a beautiful incident about dad, it left her with a warm smile of pride.

Surprisingly, despite being so close, we had never known how many lives dad had managed to touch with his aura and what he had meant to all his friends. Although we had got a hint of it from the several messages and calls that we received after dad left, but this reunion was definitely something very special. Hearing them all talk one by one did leave me as one proud daughter! By the way, I have shared some of those stories that were told to me on that sunny afternoon in Chapter 10.

One of dad's oldest friends, Shobho bhattacharya uncle, not only spoke about dad so fondly that day but he also introduced mom and me very warmly to the Modern fraternity, which felt so nice.

It was the time for the finale, the big group picture of the (1970) batch, and once again, I was given the responsibility to get everyone together and get them ready for the picture. As I helped everyone stand according to their height, my heart searched for dad so badly. This picture looked so incomplete without him, and moreover, the fact that his own daughter was making it happen broke me even more. They all looked so nice and happy, and they assembled as per my instructions so sweetly. I asked mom to sit in the middle where I imagined dad would have sat. As the camera clicked, silent tears flowed from mom's and my eyes, and then, I decided to jump in the frame and got one last picture done with all of them in the memory of my great dad. After all, this celebration was only for him and because of him!

As the afternoon came to an end, they all left, leaving behind so many blessings and wishes for me and promised to always keep in touch as they all felt I reminded them so much of my dad. I may never be even 10 percent of him, but when they said so, it surely made my heart swell up with so much pride that it more than made up for the tears that I had shed during that afternoon, hiding in corners here and there and behind my dark sunglasses.

Dad's reunion left me with some very important lessons for life. It somehow felt that life came around in a full circle;

it felt that it was one of those tasks left incomplete by him and God helped me complete it for him to bring him happiness.

All of dad's friends that day saw a lot of strength in me, whereas I saw no choice. It had nothing to do with inner strength, not that I had moved on or my grief as over, but it just happened like that; perhaps dad wanted it this way. Like it, many more unfinished dreams will appear in days, months and years to come, and I will try my best to fullfill them. I may not be as competent and amazing like him, but I can surely try as I will always have him in me, and I am sure he will always be around, guiding me and blessing me. When you lose something, you also receive something in return. When I lost dad, I lost the blanket of protection, but I definitely inherited his values that will be with me for a lifetime. Every time I look up in the sky, I feel he is looking over me as my guiding angel, my north star!

Many times, I feel like turning back and saying, "I know, dad, you did it." Just when I was beginning to lose the direction of my book, not knowing on what note and how to end it, dad gave me signs and direction; he helped me with the perfect closure on not only on my feelings but also for the book, turning the sadness in my words, feelings of extreme grief and tears into strong belief in growth, healing and, most importantly, gratitude.

Life won't ever be the same again, but I am sure we will learn to live again and even smile. Today, some memories bring back so much pain and tears, the thought of him breaks me and his mention explodes a volcano of emotions so often, but as days, months and years will pass, I am sure God will give me the courage to learn to celebrate the life he lived and the man he was.

I remember when he left, I only had anger and grief. I was full of resentment and denial, my religious beliefs were totally shaken. In fact, even after months of losing him, I still can't pray and chant the way I used to at one point of time, but I'll surely wait to heal slowly, day by day, with each experience, because I know no matter how bad the situation had been, my dad was God's favourite. I had always heard that good people go first as God loves them and wants them to be around him. My dad was one of them, a special soul! Even in the worst times of the pandemic, God didn't deny dad anything. When people were struggling even for basic necessities and medical help, God made everything available for dad in the blink of an eye; we would think of it, and it would be made available, be it medicines, tests, ambulance, hospital bed, ICU, strongest steroids and even the crematorium. God didn't make dad wait for anything at all. In fact, he was so eager to have my dad with him that he didn't let his favourite child suffer at all! I had heard shocking stories from all over Delhi at that time, and one such story involved a famous Delhi journalist. She had struggled to get her covid-positive dad a hospital bed, and later, she even had to fight hard for a crematorium spot. I just felt so thankful to God that we didn't have to experience any of it at all. Even though his departure was so painful and untimely, the journey was as smooth as one could have had in those most challenging times this generation could have ever witnessed.

As a daughter, I may never accept God's divine will, but I will respect it and learn to live with what he left behind. Losing a parent at any stage of life is painful. It does not matter how much time you get to spend with them, it is never enough. No child would ever be able to accept this loss with grace. But thanks to my extraordinary father, I got more than what I deserved, even in these few years of being together, and it will be enough for me to make peace at some point in this lifetime, if not today.

Just like the other day, I realised there were so many questioned left unanswered by dad! I had so much more to ask him about life and dealing with people and situations. I always thought I didn't need to hurry; he was right there, just a call away, and I could always ask him anytime. But today, my queries go unanswered as it is too late! There are days I feel like looking back and asking dad how he would have dealt with the situation had he been in my place. It still amazes me how effortlessly he used to react to situations and deal with them, unlike most of us who react so differently. No wonder he had won over so many people and formed such valuable relationships that mattered above money and materialistic gains.

I will miss growing old with him. He will be remembered on every big and small occasion, on every festival and event. I'll remember him when I watch his favourite movie or hear his favourite song, eat butter chicken or *badam halwa*. I'll missing having new pictures and new memories with him. I'll miss sharing my happiness and sorrows with him. I will miss receiving my morning messages and *rajnigandha* flowers on my birthdays. I will miss him lecturing me to slow down as I am growing old! I will miss him in every milestone that my daughter Manya crosses in her life without her *nanu's* blessings for he was her biggest cheerleader.

Maybe slowly, I will learn to celebrate him too! Dress up like he would want me to; host the best parties like he used to throw with an open heart. Do everything that would make me feel that he is still around. I may never get closures on my feelings, but maybe, one day my heart would learn to believe that the kind of blessed soul he was he surely deserved to be in a better and purer world than this, beautiful and stress free.

Every time I walk a lonely path, I will look to hold his hand tight for guidance. Sometimes, my heart wonders what if by now dad was reborn; where he would be; where his soul must have landed and in which body; and many such questions that would never find their answers. The year 2021 took away so much that it will never be forgotten. It took away my biggest strength, my biggest happiness and that big permanent smile on my face was gone, but it gave me this book, a memoir for life, a medium to meet my own dad once again in a way I never knew was even possible. Every time I will flip through the pages, he will just come alive in front of me, especially when the memories will begin to fade. In some way, I am grateful to 2021 for making me realise that I had dad in my life for all those lovely years. I made myself understand that I lived more years with him in my life than the ones without him, but I will always regret when another year in my life will be added without him. I now have my precious mom to look after and nurture just the way dad would have done. I will hold her extremely close to my heart as she is all that I have now.

This year gave me responsibilities that I never thought I was competent enough to handle and left a lot of life lessons. The realisation of moving toward 2022 without dad, at one point, felt so impossible. As the new year's eve approached, it felt that I was leaving behind my beloved dad in the past. For families like us that were still grieving, new year didn't feel like a fresh start at all. The new year 2022 made me feel like I was getting further away from my dad. At least in 2021, I had him, had his presence, but in this new year, I won't have him at all, no new memories of him. Moreover, the new year reminded me of how much time had passed by without dad in our lives now. It felt like I wouldn't even manage to take on more step, but then, I decided to keep it going and channel dad's spirit and energy in everything that I do in 2022, as that would be the best gift I could give to my beloved dad.

Just as I was about to finish the manuscript and hand it over for the publishing process, I tested COVID-positive and that too on 1 January 2022! Delhi was now facing the third wave at its peak. When the report came, I was shattered. For a second, I thought could it really be happening to me. It felt like all that I was trying to leave behind was coming back again, but as I collected my emotions and tried to cool down, I felt there was a strong force that was backing me and protecting me all the time. This was the ME time that I perhaps needed badly since so long. All these months that passed by actually took a toll on my mental and physical health and I had no time for myself at all. I got this time to do the final editing of my manuscript, which I just wasn't able to do in last 15 days as everyone in the house wanted a piece of my attention all the time. As I sit alone in isolation, just one week before my fortieth birthday and write these few last lines, I hope I am able to recover fast and see all of you at the launch of my dear dad's memoir, to celebrate the man that he was and the beautiful life he had lived.

I have decided to move forward in his name and do good things on this earth in his honour. It may never reduce the pain of losing him but it will surely give me a direction as I journey through the waves of grief.

And when we meet again, I hope to hear him say, "Thank you for continuing my life story."

Mom and me at dad's 50th year reunion at modern school

Author Bio

Born and brough-up in Delhi, Divya Gupta Kotawala wears several hats — she is a wife, a mother to a 14-year-old girl Mnaya, co-owner of a Delhi-based jewellery brand, House of Kotawala, along with her husband Manish and a loyal friend to a bunch of quadragenarian, whom she has known for nearly four decades! However, the role that she has cherished the most in her life is that of the daughter of her father, Shri Suresh Gupta. Divya lost her father to COVID in 2021.

Divya completed her schooling from Modern School, Barakhamba Road, where she excelled in numerous extracurricular activities and won many awards of appreciation and recognition throughout. Later, she joined the prestigious St. Stephen's College, Delhi University, where she did her honours in History. Thereafter, in pursuit of her passion for designing and creativity, Divya joined the National Institute of Fashion Technology (NIFT) for a course in fashion designing. And post that she tried a few freelance projects and partnered in a kids oriented development and enhancement project Yellow Bumble with a friend. After this, she went to join her husband in a 300-year-old family business and is currently occupied with the same.

For Divya, life has been all about simplicity, creativity and maintaining a healthy balance between her personal, professional and social life. Divya also has a strong spiritual side; she enjoys chanting and is an ardent follower of *Guruji*. It helps her maintain her peace and stay calm in any situation that life gets her into.

A once super happy and fun person, Divya fell into a deep ditch of mourning and grief after losing her beloved dad. She feels that she has found her true calling and purpose through this book that made her revisit her oldest passion of writing and communicating her feelings and emotions through words to not only to her Hero in heaven, but also with the world.

Epilogue

A special poem very close to Dad's heart.

Dad recited this poem at the inter-house poetry competition when in school, in 1968, and won the prize for best poetry recitation. Years later, he again recited the same poem during the online celebration of his 50th year reunion in 2020.

Eventually, it became the last voice note that we now have of him – a very special one and was even played during his online farewell that was done by MSOSA in his memory, in May 2021.

Ji haan hujoor, main geet bechataa hoon.

main tarah-tarah ke

geet bechataa hoon;

main kisim-kisim ke geet

bechataa hoon.

Ji, maal dekhie daam bataaoongaa,
bekaam nahiin hai, kaam bataaoongaa;
kuchh geet likhe hain masti men mainne,
kuchh geet likhe hain pasti men mainne;
yah geet, sakht saradard bhulaayegaa;
yah geet piyaa ko paas bulaayegaa.
Ji, pahale kuchh din sharm lagii mujh ko
par piichhe-piichhe akl jagii mujh ko;
Ji, logon ne to bech diye iimaan.
Ji, aap n hon sun kar jyaadaa hairaan.
main soch-samajhakar aakhir
apane geet bechataa hoon;
Ji haan hujoor, main geet bechataa hoon.

yah geet subah kaa hai, gaa kar dekhen,
yah geet gjb kaa hai, Dhaa kar dekhe;
yah geet jraa soone men likhaa thaa,
yah geet vahaan poone men likhaa thaa.
yah geet pahaaDii par chaDh jaataa hai
yah geet baDhaaye se baDh jaataa hai
yah geet bhookh aur pyaas bhagaataa hai
Ji, yah masaan men bhookh jagaataa hai;
yah geet bhuvaalii kii hai havaa hujoor

yah geet tapedik kii hai davaa hujoor.
main siidhe-saadhe aur aTapaTe
geet bechataa hoon;
Ji haan hujoor, main geet bechataa hoon.

Ji, aur geet bhii hain, dikhalaataa hoon
Ji, sunanaa chaahen aap to gaataa hoon;
Ji, chhand aur be-chhand pasand karen –
Ji, amar geet aur ve jo turat maren.
naa, buraa maanane kii isamen kyaa baat,
main paas rakhe hoon klam aur daavaat
inamen se bhaaye nahiin, naye likh doon ?
in dinon kii duharaa hai kavi-dhandhaa,
hain donon chiije vyast, kalam, kandhaa.
kuchh ghanTe likhane ke, kuchh ferii ke
Ji, daam nahiin loongaa is derii ke.
main naye puraane sabhii tarah ke
geet bechataa hoon.
Ji haan, hujoor, main geet bechataa hoon.

Ji geet janam kaa likhoon, maraN kaa likhoon;
Ji, geet Jit kaa likhoon, sharaN kaa likhoon;
yah geet reshamii hai, yah khaadii kaa,

yah geet pitt kaa hai, yah baadii kaa.
kuchh aur Dijaayan bhii hain, ye ilmii –
yah liije chalatii chiij nayii, filmii.
yah soch-soch kar mar jaane kaa geet,
yah dukaan se ghar jaane kaa geet,
Ji nahiin dillagii kii is men kyaa baat
main likhataa hii to rahataa hoon din-raat.
to tarah-tarah ke ban jaate hain geet,
Ji rooTh-ruTh kar man jaate hai geet.
Ji bahut Dher lag gayaa haTaataa hoon
gaahak kii marJi – achchhaa, jaataa hoon.
main bilakul antim aur dikhaataa hoon –
yaa bhiitar jaa kar poochh aaiye, aap.
hai geet bechanaa vaise bilakul paap
kyaa karoon magar laachaar haar kar
geet bechataa han.
Ji haan hujoor, main geet bechataa hoon.

– Bhawani Prasad Mishra

Dad
You will live in my heart forever
Divya

www.ingramcontent.com/pod-product-compliance
Lightning Source LLC
Chambersburg PA
CBHW020838120726
48008CB00001B/3

* 9 7 9 8 8 9 4 7 5 6 6 4 6 *